sing a song *of* poetry

A Teaching Resource for Phonemic Awareness, Phonics, and Fluency

D1129419

1. Make one copy of the poem as a master.

2. Fold the Suggestions up out of sight before making copies for your children.

fold here

3. Make copies for children to use in class or share with their families.

This reproducible, one-per-page format enables you to share (when appropriate) printed copies of the poems with your children after you've worked with and enjoyed the poems together in class.

FirstHand
An imprint of Heinemann
A division of Reed Elsevier Inc.
361 Hanover Street
Portsmouth, NH 03801–3912
www.firsthand.heinemann.com

Offices and agents throughout the world

© 2004 by Gay Su Pinnell and Irene C. Fountas

All rights reserved. No part of this book may be reproduced in any form or by any electronic or mechanical means, including information storage and retrieval systems, without permission in writing from the publisher, except by a reviewer, who may quote brief passages in a review.

Library of Congress Cataloging-in-Publication Data

CIP data is on file with the Library of Congress.

ISBN 0-325-00655-5

Printed in the United States of America on acid-free paper

07 06 05 04   ML   2 3 4 5 6

Sing a Song of Poetry

A Teaching Resource for Phonemic Awareness, Phonics, and Fluency

Introduction

Sing a Song of Poetry rolls off the tongue and moves the heart and spirit, if not the feet and hands. Rhythmical language of any sort delights young children as it surrounds them with the magical sounds of dancing words. But poetry, verse and song provide the magic of teaching as well; indeed, oral language is the doorway to the world of written language and the foundation for literacy. As kindergartners respond to the sound patterns, intriguing words, and inspiring ideas they find in poems, songs, and rhymes, they are learning invaluable lessons about the ways in which our language works – knowledge that will serve them well as they become readers and writers.

The poems, songs, and rhymes in this volume are a rich source of language, ideas, and imagery that will help kindergarten children use and enjoy oral and written language. This volume is a companion to the lessons described in *Phonics Lessons, Grade K: Letters, Words, and How They Work* (Pinnell and Fountas 2003, Heinemann). It can also be used as a stand-alone resource for language and literacy opportunities in any early childhood or primary classroom.

Experiences with poetry help children become aware of the phonological system of language and provide a foundation for matching sounds with letters, letter clusters, and word parts. You can use poems, chants, and songs to help children:

► Listen for and identify rhyming words.

► Connect words that have the same beginning, ending, or medial sound.

► Begin to match sounds to letters in words.

► Introduce the culture, traditional language, and rhythmic patterns of nursery rhymes.

► Stimulate and enrich language development.

► Promote phonemic awareness by helping them notice words, syllables, rhymes, and beginning and ending sounds.

► Enhance oral language skills.

► Instill an appreciation of poetry and prose.

► Build vocabulary.

► Experience meaningful print.

- ► Participate in fluent phrased reading.
- ► Build meaningful concepts about print.
- ► Introduce letters and set the scene for letter recognition.
- ► Provide a base from which to explore writing.

Young children love poetry with rhythm and rhyme; the language of poetry sings inside their heads. As they grow older, they will learn to appreciate poetry without rhyme, but rhymes and songs are the staple of early childhood and for good reason.

Poetry provides resources for the heart and spirit. Immersing children in simple poetry at an early age instills a lifelong habit of enjoying language and seeking out poetry in order to expand one's vision. Poetry joins us to the past and to our fellow human beings in the present.

VALUES AND GOALS OF POETRY IN KINDERGARTEN CLASSROOMS

Poetry expands children's oral language abilities as it:

▶ Provides texts that are easy to remember.

▶ Builds a repertoire of the unique patterns and forms of language.

▶ Helps children become sensitive to and enjoy the sounds of language—rhymes, alliteration, assonance, onomatopoeia (buzz, whiz, woof).

▶ Supports articulation and elocution.

▶ Extends listening and speaking vocabularies.

▶ Expands knowledge of the complex syntax of language.

▶ Encourages children to manipulate and play with language.

▶ Develops phonological awareness (rhyme, syllables, onsets and rimes).

▶ Develops phonemic awareness (the ability to manipulate individual sounds).

▶ Makes it easy for children to isolate and identify sounds, take words apart, and change sounds in words to make new words.

▶ Provides rich examples of comparisons such as similes and metaphors.

Poetry expands children's written language abilities as it:

▶ Gives them access to memorable language that they can then match up with print.

▶ Expands spoken vocabulary, making it easier later for them to read words.

▶ Helps them notice aspects of print.

▶ Provides opportunities to learn and recognize words that rhyme, end the same, start the same, or sound the same in the middle.

▶ Helps them begin to notice the letters and letter patterns associated with sounds.

▶ Provides a setting in which to develop the concept of a word and notice how spaces are used to define words in written language.

▶ Provides models of fluent reading helping children get the feel of it.

Poetry expands children's content knowledge as it:

▶ Provides new perceptions and ideas for them to think about.

▶ Helps them develop conceptual understanding.

▶ Encourages them to develop a sense of humor.

▶ Sensitizes them to the forms and style of poetry.

Poetry contributes to children's social knowledge and skills as it:

▶ Provides artistic and aesthetic experiences.

▶ Creates a sense of community through enjoying rhymes and songs as a group.

▶ Gives them access to English-speaking culture.

▶ Provides a window to many other cultures.

▶ Provides a common language for a group of children to share.

▶ Creates memories of shared enjoyable times.

The Elements of Poetry

The following unique elements provide the essence of poetry's appeal. In the poems appropriate for young children, language patterns, rhyme, rhythm, and humor dominate, but all the elements are present.

RHYME

While not all poems rhyme, many of the simple poems children enjoy include words that have alliterative beginning parts *(onsets)* and/or assonant ending parts *(rimes)*. The *onset* of a syllable is the consonant or consonant cluster that starts the word. The *rime* is the vowel and everything after the first part. So the onset of *pig* is *p,* and the rime is *ig.* The onset of *big* is *b,* and the rime is *ig.* The words *pig* and *big* rhyme, because they have the same rime (but remember, rime and rhyme refer to the sound rather than the spelling).

Think about this traditional rhyme:

Little Miss Muffet

Sat on a tuffet

Eating her curds and whey.

Along came a spider,

And sat down beside her,

And frightened Miss Muffet away!

The words *Muffet* and *tuffet* have different onsets but the same rime (uff) followed by the same syllable (et). Likewise, *whey* and *away* are related, with *away* having an extra syllable at the beginning. They also have two different (and very hard to distinguish) onsets (*wh* and *w*) but the same rime (long *a*). In most oral language dialects, *spider* and *beside her* have the same rime. A reciter of this nursery rhyme is likely to pronounce the words to be sure that *spider* and *beside her* rhyme. Rhyme is appealing and memorable; *rhyme* always refers to the sound of the ending part of the word. Many of us can recall simple rhymes that we learned as children.

Rhythm

The "beat," or rhythm, of poetry brings delight to young children as they chant rhymes and songs in unison, and it helps them remember them. Both rhyme and rhythm make it easy for children to recite, remember, and eventually read fluently. Take "Giddyup" for example:

Giddyup, giddyup,

One, two, three.

Giddyup, giddyup,

Come see me.

Figurative Language

As young children internalize poetry, they respond to the sensory images. Poetry presents comparisons (similes and metaphors), as in this simple rhyme, which you no doubt remember:

Twinkle, twinkle, little star,

How I wonder what you are!

Up above the world so high,

Like a diamond in the sky.

Twinkle, twinkle, little star,

How I wonder what you are!

Often rhymes, chants, and songs contain onomatopoetic language (words like *whoosh* that sound like the phenomenon they represent). Take this example from "The Wheels on the Bus":

The wipers on the bus

Go swish, swish, swish,

Swish, swish, swish,

Swish, swish, swish.

The wipers on the bus

Go swish, swish, swish,

All through the town.

LANGUAGE PATTERNS

Rhymes and poems are most enjoyable because of the language patterns that are included. *Alliteration*, the repetition of consonant sounds, is evident in this familiar nursery rhyme, for example:

Georgy Porgy, pudding and pie,

Kissed the girls and made them cry.

When the boys came out to play,

Georgy Porgy ran away.

Another common pattern is the repetition of vowel sounds, called *assonance*. The familiar "Jack Sprat" repeats the short *a* sound and the long *e* sound.

Jack Sprat could eat no fat.

His wife could eat no lean.

And so between them both, you see,

They licked the platter clean.

REPETITION

Many poems, particularly songs, have repeating stanzas or phrases, such as "Mary Wore a Red Dress." Notice that in the following familiar nursery rhyme, "Pease Porridge Hot," *hot, cold, in the pot,* and *nine days old* are repeated.

Pease porridge hot,

Pease porridge cold,

Pease porridge in the pot,

Nine days old.

Some like it hot,

Some like it cold,

Some like it in the pot,

Nine days old.

Rhythmic repetition like this helps children learn these rhymes easily; many have been set to music and can be sung, such as "Muffin Man."

SENSORY IMAGES

Poetry arouses the senses. Just a few words can evoke memories, form visual images, point up absurdities, and help us enter unique worlds. Many children feel they have met the lady in this nursery rhyme:

Ride a cock-horse

To Banbury Cross,

To see a fine lady

Upon a white horse;

Rings on her fingers

And bells on her toes,

She shall have music

Wherever she goes.

Important Areas of Learning for Kindergarten Children

The most important benefit of using poetry in kindergarten classrooms is children's oral language development. Through their involvement in poetry, children expand their knowledge of the vocabulary and structure of English. In addition, using poetry has profound implications for helping children learn to read and write. (See *Guided Reading: Good First Teaching for All Children*, Fountas and Pinnell, Heinemann,1996; and *Word Matters: Teaching Phonics and Spelling in the Reading/Writing Classroom*, Pinnell and Fountas, Heinemann, 1998).

Several important areas of learning form a foundation for becoming literate. Even though formal reading instruction would not occur until the second half of kindergarten, young children need to develop along all of these dimensions through the early childhood years.

PHONOLOGICAL AWARENESS

The phonological system encompasses the sounds of a language. When children hear, chant, or sing poems, they become more aware of sound patterns and how they are connected (for example, words that rhyme or start the same). Gradually, they are able to identify the individual sounds (or phonemes) in words. Called *phonemic awareness,* this ability to identify individual sounds in words is essential when children are learning to connect sounds and letters. Young children need to learn to play with language and manipulate sounds. They can:

- ▶ Listen for and identify rhyming words.

- ▶ Listen for and identify syllables within words.

- ▶ Listen for individual sounds in words.

- ▶ Identify similar sounds in words.

- ▶ Divide words into sounds.

- ▶ Blend sounds to form words.

- ▶ Match sounds and letters.

LETTER LEARNING

To be able to recognize letters, children need to distinguish the *features* that make one letter different from every other letter. The differences between letters (for example, *h* and *n*) are actually quite small, and this task requires close attention. Learning how to look at letters is essential if children are to connect letters and sounds and learn letter names. Through repeated exposure to letters in the poems they experience in shared reading, children begin to notice the letters that are embedded in print. They can:

- Notice and locate letters in words.
- Learn to find the beginning letter of a word.
- Connect words by beginning or ending letters.
- Connect words in poems to letters in their names.

PHONICS

When children notice how the sounds of language are connected to the letters, they are learning letter-sound relationships or *phonics*. Early on, young children will learn the easy-to-hear consonant sounds (beginning or ending) and easy-to-hear vowels (long vowels).

CONCEPTS ABOUT PRINT

Encounters with poetry will also help children acquire some basic understandings about how print works. For example, the "front" and "back" of a book is important information. Children who are getting oriented to the world of print begin to understand that you read left to right across a line of print and that at the end of the line, you return to the left and go, again, left to right. There is one spoken word to every printed word (defined by space on either side) in print. To read, you point to each word. Further, it is important for children to understand that letters are embedded in print and that they can identify words by the sequence of the letters. They can:

- Notice print as the carrier of the message in a text.
- Follow print from top to bottom and over pages of text.
- Follow print left to right on familiar text.
- Locate words by saying them and thinking about the first sound and letter.
- Find rhyming words.
- Locate letters and familiar words in text.

FLUENCY

Young children will become verbally fluent as they repeat poems and use the phrases, pauses, stress and intonation of the language. They will also become more fluent in picking up the print off the page as many words become more automatic and their reading vocabulary expands. They can:

- ▶ Read in phrases.
- ▶ Use expression.
- ▶ Stop at periods.
- ▶ Raise the voice at question marks.
- ▶ Read smoothly.
- ▶ Put their words together so it sounds like language.
- ▶ Recognize some words quickly.

Selecting Poetry for Young Children

Selecting poetry for children depends on your purpose. You will want to consider whether they will experience the poems orally or if you will eventually expect them to process the print. Children can listen to and recite more complex poems than they can read. Simple, engaging, repetitive poems will be easy for them to remember. Knowing poems, songs, and rhymes increases children's ability to notice the sounds of language; they learn many new words to add to their oral vocabularies. When they repeat familiar poems, they are using the *syntax* or "grammar" of written language, which is different from their everyday speech. Experiencing and internalizing this complex language sets the scene for reading and understanding the simple texts they will begin to read as well as the more complex texts they will encounter later.

If children encounter a large number of poems in kindergarten, they will begin to read with you in shared reading (using an enlarged version of the text that everyone can see). In the process, children will begin to notice characteristics of print. The first poems children encounter in shared reading should:

- ► **Be relatively short.**

- ► **Employ repetition and patterned language.**

- ► **Feature a large number of words that are easy to read.**

- ► **Present generally simple vocabulary (although children may enjoy many rhymes without knowing the precise meaning of some archaic words, such as *pease porridge*).**

- ► **Focus on concepts and ideas that are familiar (for example, visual imagery and metaphor require more of children than simple rhymes and songs).**

The poems in this book represent a gradient of difficulty. At the beginning of the year, select very simple poems, gradually increasing the level of challenge. The poems in the chart below illustrate a continuum of difficulty.

① **Simplest**	② **More Difficult**	③ **Most Difficult**
I Love Chocolate	**Hey Diddle Diddle**	**The Candle**
I love chocolate	Hey diddle diddle,	Little Nancy Etticoat
Yum, yum, yum.	The cat and the fiddle,	With a white petticoat,
I love chocolate	The cow jumped	And a red nose;
In my tum.	Over the moon;	She has no feet or hands,
	The little dog laughed	The longer she stands
	To see such sport,	The shorter she grows.
	And the dish ran	
	Away with the spoon.	

Verse 1 is both simple and short. The theme is easy; there are few syllables; there is repetition. Children can say it over and over, substituting other foods. Verse 2 has longer lines and begins a story, which is told in a longer version of this common nursery rhyme. There is some nonsensical imagery, but it is easy to grasp and the rhythm helps children learn it. Verse 3, "The Candle," evokes sensory imagery and metaphor. This riddle requires thinking beyond the actual words.

As you select poems to share, consider your children's previous experience, skill with language, and vocabulary. If you begin with easy poems and they learn them very quickly (for example, they join in and can soon repeat them independently), you can provide slightly more complex examples.

Planning for Teaching Opportunities When Revisiting a Text

As short texts, poems provide a multitude of opportunities for learning about language. At first, you will be using the poems only to expand oral language, but the experience will give children plenty of chances to:

▶ Use interesting language.

▶ Say and connect words of one, two, and three syllables.

▶ Say and connect words that rhyme or that begin alike.

▶ Say words, noticing beginning and ending sounds of consonants and consonant clusters.

▶ Say words, noticing vowel sounds.

After enjoying a poem several times, you may want to revisit the text with children to help them notice features of the print such as letters, letter patterns, or words. The following grid helps you think about the varied opportunities in some sample texts. In each box we list possible features that children can notice within a poem. You can try planning some poems out for yourself in advance or use the blank grid to keep a record of your teaching points within each poem as you make them.

WORD ANALYSIS TEACHING OPPORTUNITIES WHEN REVISITING POETRY

Title	Type of Text (e.g., limerick, tongue twister, couplet, free verse)	Phonogram Patterns (e.g., -at, -ig, -oan, -ait, -ate)	Letter-Sound (beginning or ending consonants and clusters, vowel sounds)	High Frequency Words	Other (ending consonants/clusters/ digraphs, concept words like colors and numbers, names, plurals, rhyming words, syllables, new vocabulary)
I Love Chocolate	4 line poem with rhyme pair	-um	I, ch, y, t	I, love, in, my	3 syllable word
Hey Diddle Diddle	nursery rhyme	-oon	beginning d, c, f cat-cow -sh ending long o sound	the, and, to, see	-le ending action words—jumped, laughed, ran
The Candle	riddle-nursery rhyme rhyming couplet 3rd and 6th lines rhyme	-oat -and	beginning r, n, p consonant clusters st, gr, sh, wh	a, and, with, she, no, or, she	plural ending – s double t double e
Hot Cross Buns	nursery rhyme rhythmic chant	-ot -un	beginning h, b, p consonant cluster cr	a	repetition of lines plural ending – s counting words
Pat-a-cake	nursery rhyme hand play strong rhythm	-at, -an, -ake	beginning p, b, m, c, f, m, t	a, as, can, it, and, in, the, me, for, you, with	possessive – 's ending bake-baker

WORD ANALYSIS TEACHING OPPORTUNITIES WHEN REVISITING POETRY

Title	Type of Text (e.g., limerick, tongue twister, couplet, free verse)	Phonogram Patterns (e.g., -at, -ig, -oan, -ait, -ate)	Letter-Sound (beginning or ending consonants and clusters, vowel sounds)	High Frequency Words	Other (ending consonants/clusters/ digraphs, concept words like colors and numbers, names, plurals, rhyming words, syllables, new vocabulary)

Tools for Using Poetry

The tools for working with poetry are simple. You will want to have them well organized and readily available for quick lessons. We suggest the following:

▶ **EASEL**

a vertical surface for displaying chart paper, or the pocket chart, that is large enough for all children to see and sturdy enough to avoid tipping.

▶ **POCKET CHART**

a stiff piece of cardboard or plastic that has lines with grooves into which cards can be inserted so that children can work with lines of poems and/or individual words.

▶ **MASKS**

cutout cardboard shapes designed to outline words on charts for children to use in locating words or parts of words (see templates in "Materials and Routines," *Phonics Lessons, K, Teaching Resources*).

▶ **HIGHLIGHTER TAPE**

transparent stick-on tape that can be used to emphasize words, letters, or word parts.

▶ **STICK-ON NOTES**

small pieces of paper that have a sticky backing and can temporarily be used to conceal words or parts of words so that children can attend to them.

▶ **FLAGS**

a handle with a flat piece of wood or cardboard on the end that can be placed under a word on a chart as a way to locate or emphasize it (see template in "Materials and Routines," *Phonics Lessons, K, Teaching Resources*).

▶ **TAGS**

signs with concise directions so that children can remember an independent work activity; for example: *Read, Mix, Fix, Read* (*Read* the poem, *Mix* up the sentence strips of a poem, *Fix* the poem back together, and *Read* it again to check it).

▶ **ART MATERIALS**

media such as paint, glue, colored paper, tissue paper.

Instructional Contexts for Poetry

Poetry fits well into the range of activities typical in kindergarten classrooms (see Fountas and Pinnell 1996).

INTERACTIVE READ-ALOUD

Reading aloud forms a foundation for language and literacy development, and poetry is meant to be read orally. In addition, reading aloud provides a model of fluent, phrased reading. There are many wonderful picture books that present rhyming verse to children in a very engaging way. *The Itsy Bitsy Spider* (Trapani 1993) is an illustrated variation of the familiar verse. *Pignic* (Miranda 1996) is a wonderful rhyming (and repetitive consonant sounds) alphabet book in which a family of twenty-six pigs enjoy a picnic with all kinds of food. *Chicka Chicka Boom Boom* (Martin and Archambault 1989) is another rhyming alphabet book with wonderful rhythm and a focus on uppercase and lowercase letters. You can also read individual poems from volumes such as *Tomie dePaola's Mother Goose Favorites* (1985) or Kay Chorao's *Knock at the Door* (1999), a book of action rhymes.

We recommend repeated readings of favorite poems or rhyming books; it takes many repetitions for children to be able to join in. Ask them to listen the first two or three times you read a verse, but encourage them to join in after they have grasped enough to say it with you, especially on a refrain. In this way, children will begin to internalize much of the language and enjoy it more and will also get the feeling of participating in fluent, phrased reading.

SHARED READING

Shared reading involves children in both hearing the verse and seeing the print. You use an enlarged text—a chart that you have prepared or purchased or a big book. Using this shared approach allows you to demonstrate pointing while reading. After one or two repetitions, encourage children to read with you in an interactive read-aloud. Be sure that all children can see the visual display of print. You'll want to sit or stand to the side and use a thin pointer (pointers that have objects like "hands" on the end usually block children's view of the very word you are pointing out). The idea is to maximize children's attention to the print. Shared reading helps them learn how the eyes work in reading. They'll also learn more about rhyme and rhythm.

CHORAL READING AND PERFORMANCE

Choral reading is a more sophisticated version of shared reading. Participants may read from an enlarged text, but often they have their own individual copies. They may have a leader, but it is not always necessary for the leader to point to the words. Participants can practice reading together several times and then perform the piece. You can assign "solo" lines, boys' and girls' lines, question and response lines, or ask the whole group to read all the lines. Emphasize varying the voice to suit the meaning of the poem. You can add sound effects (wooden sticks, bells, or other simple tools) or simply invite children clap or snap their fingers to accentuate words or phrases.

INDEPENDENT READING

Children love reading poetry, searching for favorite poems, and illustrating poems. A personal poetry book or anthology becomes a treasure. After poems have been read in shared reading, you can reproduce them on smaller pieces of paper. Children glue the poems into a composition book or spiral notebook and illustrate them. Be sure that you are using poems that they are familiar with and can read. Reading their personal poetry books is a good independent reading activity. You'll want to use nursery rhymes and very simple poems for kindergarten children and guide the process.

WRITING POETRY

Children can begin to get a feel for writing verse through interactive writing. In interactive writing, you and the children compose a message together. You act as a scribe, using the easel, but occasionally children come up and write in a word or letter when you want to draw attention to it (See *Interactive Writing: How Language and Literacy Come Together, K–2,* McCarrier, Pinnell, and Fountas, Heinemann, 2000).

You can substitute their names in a verse or create a variation of one of their favorites (for example, for "I Love Chocolate," substitute all of their favorite foods). This activity gives them power over language, and they may want to experiment on their own.

Types of Poetry

Poetry can be categorized in many different ways—by pattern, structure, or topic, for example. This book includes rhymes and poems under the headings discussed below, which are related to both forms and themes. Many of the poems could be placed in more than one category.

NURSERY RHYMES

Traditional rhymes by anonymous poets have been passed down over generations. There are often many different versions. Originally serving as political satire for adults, they have been loved by children for generations. They usually rhyme in couplets or alternating lines and are highly rhythmic. Young children enjoy these simple verses, and they help to build a foundation that will later lead them to a more sophisticated appreciation of poetry. The "Mother Goose" rhymes, which were published in the eighteenth century, are the best known, but equivalents exist around the world. An example children love is "Humpty Dumpty":

Humpty Dumpty sat on a wall,

Humpty Dumpty had a great fall;

All the king's horses, and all the king's men,

Couldn't put Humpty together again.

RHYMED VERSE

Many poems for young children have lines that end with words that rhyme. These may be rhyming couplets (each pair of lines rhyme), as in "Cobbler, Cobbler":

Cobbler, cobbler, mend my shoe.

Get it done by half past two;

Stitch it up and stitch it down,

Then I'll give you half a crown.

Or, every other line may rhyme, as in "Peas":

I eat my peas with honey,

I've done it all my life.

It makes the peas taste funny,

But it keeps them on the knife.

There are a variety of other rhyming patterns such as in "I Scream":

I scream.

You scream.

We all scream

For ice cream!

FREE VERSE (UNRHYMED)

Many poems evoke sensory images and sometimes have rhythm but do not rhyme. Haiku poems, for example, have a defined number of syllables; these "spare" poems evoke visual images. An example is "Snow," by Issa:

I could eat it!

This snow that falls

So softly, so softly.

Children will also enjoy all the different adjectives and actions applied to sand in "The Beach":

White sand,

Sea sand,

Warm sand,

Kicking sand,

Building sand,

Watching sand

As the waves roll in.

Here's an example of an action verse that has rhythm but does not rhyme—"I Have a Little Wagon":

I have a little wagon, [*hold hand out, palm up*]

It goes everywhere with me [*move hand around*]

I can pull it [*pull hand in*]

I can push it [*push hand away*]

I can turn it upside down [*turn hand upside down*]

WORD PLAY

Some poems play with words by juxtaposing interesting word patterns in a humorous and playful way, like "Willaby, Wallaby, Woo":

Willaby, wallaby, woo,

An elephant stepped on you.

Willaby, wallaby, wee,

An elephant stepped on me.

In word play we also include tongue twisters (poems that play with words in a way that makes them very difficult to recite without stumbling because the words are difficult to pronounce one after another). A well-known example is:

Fuzzy Wuzzy was a bear.

Fuzzy Wuzzy had no hair.

Fuzzy Wuzzy wasn't fuzzy,

Was he?

HUMOROUS VERSE

Humorous verse draws children's attention to absurdities as well as to the sounds and rhythms of language. Sometimes these humorous verses tell stories—for example, "There Once Was a Queen":

There once was a queen
Whose face was green.
She ate her milk
And drank her bread,
And got up in the morning
To go to bed.

SONGS

Songs are musical texts originally intended to be sung. An example is "Polly Put the Kettle On":

Polly put the kettle on,
Polly put the kettle on,
Polly put the kettle on,
We'll all have tea.

Sukey take it off again,
Sukey take it off again,
Sukey take it off again,
They've all gone away.

You may know the traditional tunes to the songs we have included in this volume, but if you don't, you can compose your own or simply have children chant them, enjoying the rhythm and rhyme.

ACTION SONGS AND POEMS

Action poems involve action along with rhythm and rhyme. An example is "Pease Porridge":

Pease porridge hot, [*clap own hands*]

Pease porridge cold, [*clap partner's hands*]

Pease porridge in the pot, [*clap own hands*]

Nine days old. [*clap partner's hands*]

Some like it hot, [*one fist on top of the other*]

Some like it cold, [*alternate fists, placing the other on top*]

Some like it in the pot, [*clap partner's hands*]

Nine days old. [*clap own hands*]

This category also includes jump-rope songs, traditional rhymes that children originally chanted while they jumped rope. An example is "Teddy Bear, Teddy Bear":

Teddy bear, teddy bear,

Turn around.

Teddy bear, teddy bear,

Touch the ground.

Children can chant and act out jump-rope songs. There are also chants that accompany games or are simply enjoyable to say together. Chants, like songs, showcase rhythm and rhyme.

CONCEPT POEMS

Poems in this category focus on concepts such as numbers, days of the week, colors, ordinal words, seasons, and any other category of information. An example is "Five Little Ducks Went In For a Swim":

Five little ducks went in for a swim;

The first little duck put his head in.

The second little duck put his head back;

The third little duck said, "Quack, quack, quack."

The fourth little duck with his tiny brother

Went for a walk with his father and mother.

This poem contains ordinal words (*first, second, third, fourth*) and the synonyms *little* and *tiny*.

These verses are not only engaging but also easy to learn. As children learn them, they will be repeating the vocabulary that surrounds important concepts.

In the category of concept poems, we also include name poems, which really transcend categories. Many verses present a wonderful opportunity to substitute children's names for names or words already there. In "Pat-a-cake," you can substitute different children's names (and their first letters) for *Tommy*. Some of the names will not rhyme with *me,* but children will not mind. There are other rhymes included in this collection, with blank lines for children to fill in their names. "Come, Butter, Come," "Rain, Rain, Go Away" and "Who is Wearing Red?" are some examples.

Many of the verses in the book also offer similar innovations, so look for opportunities. Children will love substituting their own words and phrases. They will develop ownership for the writing and become more sensitive to rhymes, syllables, and word patterns in the process.

Fifty Ways to Use Poems—Plus!

Below we suggest fifty specific ways to use the poems in this volume. Plus, you will notice that each poem includes an instructional suggestion—an easy way to refine and extend the learning and enjoyment potential of each poem. You will find many more ways to engage your children in joyful play with oral and written language. The rich collection of poems in this volume can be reproduced, analyzed, or simply read aloud. Enjoy!

Decisions about using poetry depend on your purposes for instruction and the age of your children. By going over favorites again and again, children will internalize rhymes and develop awareness of new language structures. They will become more sensitive to the sounds of language and take pleasure in it. In kindergarten, you will want to phase in more attention to print, but be sure to enjoy the poem several times before working on the details. Try out some of the following as appropriate to kindergarten:

1. MARCHING TO RHYMES	Marching around the room while chanting a poem will help children feel the rhythm.
2. FLANNELBOARDS	Make flannelboard figures for favorite nursery rhyme characters. Children can say the rhyme as they move figures around. You can also glue felt or attach Velcro to the back of pictures that students have drawn on card stock.
3. STORYBOARDS	Have students draw or paint a backdrop that represents the scene from a rhyme or song. Then have them make cutout figures and glue them on popsicle sticks so that they can move the puppets around in front of the backdrop.
4. LISTENING FOR RHYMES	Have children clap or snap their fingers when they come to a rhyming word. They can also say the rhyming word softer (or louder) or mouth the word without making a sound.
5. RESPONDING	Divide the class in half. Taking a familiar poem, have half the group read (or say) the poem up to the rhyming word and then stop. Let the other half of the class shout the rhyming word.
6. POEMS ON TAPE	Record specific poems on a tape so that children can listen independently at a listening center. Include card stock copies of the poems, and show children how to follow along with the recording.

7. CLASS POETRY TAPE	As children learn poems, gradually add to a class tape of their poetry reading or chanting. Keep a table of contents for the tape on a chart and/or place the taped poems in a book. Children can listen to the tape while following along in the book.
8. POEM PICTURES	After reading a poem aloud at different times of the day, have children make pictures to go with it and display them with the poem. Duplicate individual copies of a simple poem and ask each child to illustrate it.
9. WORD ENDINGS	Write the poem in large print on a chart or on strips for a pocket chart. After many readings of a poem on a large chart, help children notice words that rhyme and specific vocabulary. They can use a masking card or highlighter tape to mark these words.
10. POEM INNOVATIONS	Engage children in noticing and using the language syntax in the poem to create their own similar versions. For example, insert different names in "Jack Be Nimble" or different foods in "I Like Chocolate."
11. PERSONAL POETRY BOOKS	Have children make their own personal poetry books by gluing the poems they have experienced in shared reading into spiral notebooks and then illustrating them. Over time they will have a large personal collection of poems to take home.
12. LITTLE POEM BOOKS	Make individual poem books, with one line of a poem on each page (for example, "One, two, buckle my shoe"); children can illustrate each page, read the book, and take it home.
13. POEM PERFORMANCES	Children can perform the poems after they learn them, sometimes adding sound effects with rhythm instruments such as sticks and drums or by clapping and snapping their fingers.
14. RESPONSIVE READING	Find poems such as "Are You Sleeping?" that lend themselves to recitation by two or more speakers. Groups of children read questions and answers or alternate lines.
15. POETRY PLAY	Lead children in saying their favorite poems while they line up, as they walk through an area in which their talking will not disturb other classes, or any time they have a moment or two of "wait time."

16. Line-up poems	When passing out of the room for recess or lunch, play games in which children say or finish a line of a poem in order to take their place in line.
17. Rhyming cloze	Read poems, asking children to join in only on the rhyming words. Put highlighter tape on the rhyming words.
18. Finger poems and action poems	Make finger plays from poems. Do poems with motions involving the entire body. We have included finger-play and action directions for many poems, but you can make up many more.
19. Poem posters	Use art materials (colored and/or textured paper, pens, crayons, paints) to illustrate poems on charts for the whole group to enjoy, or individually in personal poetry books.
20. Poems with blanks	Give children individual copies of poems with a blank space in which they can write their names (or you can write it for them).
21. Mystery words	In shared reading of a familiar poem, leave out key words but put in the first letter so that children can check their reading.
22. Poem displays	Display a poem in several places in the room; children find the poem and use chopstick pointers to read it in small and large versions in different places.
23. Poetry box	Make a poetry box that contains slightly enlarged and illustrated versions of familiar poems; children can take them out and read them to a buddy.
24. Poetry board	Make a theme poetry board using poems that explore a concept (for example, animals or vegetables).
25. Tongue twisters	Make up tongue twisters using the names of children in the class and have them illustrate the verses; for example Carol carries cookies, carrots, candy, and cucumbers in a cart.
26. Pocket chart	Place poems on sentence strips in a pocket chart for a variety of activities: • Substituting words to innovate on the text; • Highlighting words, letters, or parts of words with colored transparent plastic or highlighter tape; • Putting sentence strips in order and reading; • Masking words; • Placing cards over words to predict and then check predictions with the print.

27. POEM PUZZLES

Have the children cut a poem into strips, mix them up, order them, and glue them on paper in the correct order. Then have them use art materials to illustrate the text. You can create a simple strip template to photocopy for many different poems.

28. CLASS POEM OR SONG BOOKS

Take one simple familiar poem and put each line on one page of an oversized class book. Staple the book together. Children can illustrate it and read it to others.

29. SEQUENCING POEMS

Once they have internalized a poem, kindergarteners can write one line of a simple poem on separate pages, staple the pages together as a book, illustrate the pages, and then read the book to others.

30. MORE SONGS AND POEMS

Be on the alert for popular songs that children like or street rhymes that they know. Take appropriate verses from these songs and add them to the poetry collection.

31. POEM PLAYS

Create a "play" from the poem. Read the poem (children may join in) while several children act it out.

32. POETRY DRESS-UP

Collect some simple "dress up" items related to the rhymes and poems in your collection. Invite the children to dress up for the poem reading.

33. POETRY PARTY

Have a party to which everyone comes dressed as a character from a poem. (Props may be made of paper.) The group has to guess which poem is represented and then read the poem to the child representing that character.

34. CHARACTER BULLETIN BOARD

Each child draws a favorite character from a poem and then cuts the figure out. Use interactive writing to create labels for each character on the board.

35. PUPPET SHOW

Have the children make and use finger, stick, or hand puppets to say the poem.

36. CELEBRITY POETRY TAPE

Prepare a poetry tape of the children's favorite poems, which you can place in a box in written form. Ask the principal, librarian, parents, and other teachers to read poems on the tape. Children will enjoy listening to the different voices and following the words.

37. POETRY PICNIC

Many poems have something to do with food. For example, "curds and whey" is cottage cheese. After children have learned a lot of verses, make a list of foods. Children can bring some of them or you can bring them. Then, they say the poem and eat the food.

38. POETRY PAIRS

Children find two poems that go together in some way. They bring the two poems to sharing time and tell how they are alike. You can make a class book of poem pairs with (illustrated) connected poems on opposite pages.

39. POETRY LANDSCAPE MURAL

Children paint a background on which they can glue different poetry characters. This mural requires some planning. For example, you would want a field of corn for "Little Boy Blue" or a mountain for the bear to go over.

40. POETRY SORT

Have a box of poems on cards that children know very well and can read. They can read the poems and sort them in any way they want to—theme (happy, silly, sad), topic (mice, girls, boys, bears), the way they rhyme (two lines, every other line, no rhyme).

41. POEMS IN SHAPES

Have children read a poem and then glue the poem on a shape (give them a template) that represents it. For example, "Window Watching" could be on or near a window.

42. MIXED-UP POEM

Place a familiar poem on sentence strips in the pocket chart. Mix it up and have children help you rebuild it by saying the lines and looking for the next one. You can also have a correct model displayed beside the cutup version so that they can check it. Soon children will be able to perform this action on their own.

43. PICTURE WORDS

Have children draw pictures for key words in a poem and display them right above the word on a chart.

44. HUNTING FOR WORDS

Using flyswatters with rectangular holes in the center (or masking cards), have children hunt for particular words or words that rhyme with or start like another.

45. WORD LOCATION

Have a familiar poem in the pocket chart but with some blanks. Give children some key words. Stop when you come to the key word and ask who has it. Children will need to think about beginning sounds and letters.

46. WORD MATCH

Place one line of a poem in the pocket chart and have children rebuild the line by matching individual words under the line.

47. BUILDER POEM

Give a group of children one word each of a poem, written in large print on a card. The rest of the class lines up these children so that the word order is correct. Then they take turns walking down the line and saying the poem by pointing to each child and his or her word.

48. LOOKING AT HIGH FREQUENCY WORDS

The words children encounter over and over in poems will form a core of words that they know and can recognize rapidly. You can have children locate the words to draw attention to them. They can also match word cards by placing like words on top of the words in the poem. An interesting exercise is to create high frequency words in different fonts. Be sure the words are clear and recognizable. Matching these words to words on a chart or in the pocket chart creates an additional challenge in looking at the features of letters.

49. POETRY NEWSLETTER

Send home a monthly newsletter that tells parents the poems children have learned and provides some poems they can sing or say at home.

50. CLASS POETRY BOOK

Collect favorite poems into a class book that is small enough to be portable. Children take turns taking the book home. They can read the poems to stuffed animal or family members.

Poetry Links to Phonics Lessons

In *Phonics Lessons: Letters, Words, and How They Work, Grade K,* you will find under LINK, Shared Reading recommendations that enable you to connect learning across the Language and Literacy Framework. Often, the shared reading recommendations suggest you turn to *Sing A Song of Poetry* for instructional follow-up using particular poems, songs, and verse. This list links many phonics lessons to a specific poem that extends and refines the instructional aim of the lesson; however, you will notice that not all lessons are linked to a poem and, sometimes, a lesson is linked to two or more poems. What does this mean? The links are completely flexible! Feel free to find and make your own links, and do not feel compelled to use every poem we recommend.

The primary goal of this collection is, quite literally, to "sing a song of poetry"! Invite your children to chant, recite, echo, and play with the poems. Above all, *Sing A Song of Poetry* is meant to inspire a love of language.

Early Literacy Concepts

ELC 1		ELC 5	
ELC 2	Charlie Over the Ocean; Elsie Marley; Come, Butter, Come; Who Is Wearing Red?	ELC 6	
		ELC 7	Go to Bed; Jerry Hall
ELC 3	Good Morning; Apples, Peaches	ELC 8	
ELC 4	Mary Wore Her Red Dress; Sally Go 'Round		

Phonological Awareness

PA 1	A-hunting We Will Go; Mary Had a Little Lamb	PA 15	
PA 2	Jack, Jack; Little Fishes in a Brook	PA 16	
PA 3	High and Low; Jack Sprat	PA 17	
PA 4	Bouncing Ball; Dormy, Dormy, Dormouse; Jack, Be Nimble	PA 18	Little Miss Muffet; Windshield Wiper
PA 5	I'm Dusty Bill; Ladybug! Ladybug!	PA 19	Hickory, Dickory, Dock!
PA 6	Little Jack Horner; Open, Shut Them	PA 20	
PA 7		PA 21	I'm Dusty Bill; Make a Pancake; My Dog, Rags
PA 8	Five Fat Peas; Grandpa Grig	PA 22	
PA 9		PA 23	
PA 10		PA 24	There Was an Old Woman; To Market, to Market
PA 11		PA 25	Hickory, Dickory, Dock!
PA 12	Polly Put the Kettle On; Pussycat, Pussycat	PA 26	Hickory, Dickory, Dore!; Higglety, Pigglety, Pop!
PA 13	Red, White, and Blue; Six Little Ducks		
PA 14	Stop, Look, and Listen; Stretching Fun		

Letter Knowledge

LK 1	The Alphabet Song	LK 13	
LK 2	Time to Pick Up; Tommy Snooks	LK 14	
LK 3	Two Little Houses; Window Watching	LK 15	Elizabeth, Elspeth, Betsey, and Bess; Mary Ann, Mary Ann
LK 4	Tommy Snooks; Lucy Locket	LK 16	Jumping Joan; Make a Pancake
LK 5		LK 17	
LK 6		LK 18	
LK 7	The Alphabet Song	LK 19	
LK 8	Bingo; The Alphabet Song	LK 20	
LK 9	Bouncing Ball; Cackle, Cackle, Mother Goose	LK 21	
LK 10	Puppies and Kittens; Peas	LK 22	Teeter-totter; Mix a Pancake
LK 11		LK 23	
LK 12	Johnny Taps With One Hammer; Rain, Rain, Go Away	LK 24	

Letter/Sound Relationships

LS 1	Snail, Snail; Three Blind Mice	**LS 5**	
LS 2		**LS 6**	
LS 3	This Is the Way We Wash Our Face	**LS 7**	
LS 4	Two Little Blackbirds	**LS 8**	My Little Sister; Papa's Glasses

Spelling Patterns

SP 1		**SP 5**	The Beach; If You're Happy and You Know It
SP 2	The Cat; Make a Pancake	**SP 6**	As I Was Walking; Hiccup, Hiccup; Pat-a-Cake
SP 3	Muffin Man; We Can	**SP 7**	The Elephant Goes Like This; Pease Porridge Hot;
SP 4	Five Little Snowmen; How Many Days?; Rain, Rain, Go Away		

High Frequency Words

HF 1	As I Was Going Along (*I*); I Had a Loose Tooth (*a*); Great A (*me*); I Have a Little Wagon (*it*); To Market, to Market (*to*)	**HF 5**	Billy, Billy (*come*); Jack Sprat (*no*); Sing, Sing (*do*); There Was an Old Woman (*an*); Wheels on the Bus (*go*)
HF 2	Did You Ever See a Lassie? (*and*); Fiddle-de-dee (*the*); I'm a Little Teapot (*is*); Jack-in-the-box (*in*); My Eyes Can See (*can*)	**HF 6**	Are You Sleeping? (*you*); Hey Diddle Diddle (*see*); Little Snail (*so*); Point to the Right (*up*); This Is the Way We Wash Our Face (*we*)
HF 3	Baby Mice; I Have a Little Wagon;	**HF 7**	I Clap My Hands; Little Red Apple
HF 4	Little Jack Horner (*he*); Milkman, Milkman (*my*); Pease Porridge Hot (*like*); Sometimes (*am*); Wee Willie Winkie (*at*)		

Word Meaning

WM 1	Mary Wore Her Red Dress; Red, White, and Blue	**WM 4**	Jumping Beans; One For Sorrow
WM 2	Color Song; Roses Are Red; Who Is Wearing Red?	**WM 5**	Five Little Ducks Went in for a Swim
WM 3	One Potato, Two Potato; One, Two, Buckle My Shoe; One, Two, Three, Four	**WM 6**	How Many Days?; Tommy Snooks
		WM 7	How Many Days?; Today

Word Structure

WS 1	Here Are My Ears; Hot Cross Buns	**WS 4**	Ladybug! Ladybug!; Pussycat, Pussycat; What's the Weather?
WS 2	Beets; Papa's Glasses; The Rooster		
WS 3	Bouncing Ball; Hickety, Pickety; I Stand on Tiptoe; Milkman, Milkman; Someone's Birthday		

Word Solving Actions

WSA 1		**WSA 6**	Five Little Snowmen; Go to Bed Early
WSA 2	Little Red Apple; Who Stole the Cookies?	**WSA 7**	
WSA 3		**WSA 8**	
WSA 4	The Cat; Make a Pancake	**WSA 9**	
WSA 5			

A-hunting We Will Go

Oh, a-hunting we will go,

A-hunting we will go,

We'll catch a fox and put him in a box,

And then we'll let him go.

SUGGESTION: After the children learn this song, substitute other animal names and objects that rhyme, the sillier the better: *whale–pail; skunk–trunk; snail–jail; bear–chair.*

All by Myself

These are things I can do

All by myself.

I can comb my hair and fasten my shoe

All by myself.

I can wash my hands and wash my face

All by myself.

I can put my toys and blocks in place

All by myself.

ACTIONS:
These are things I can do
All by myself. [*point to self*]
I can comb my hair and fasten my shoe [*point to hair and shoe*]
All by myself. [*point to self*]
I can wash my hands and wash my face [*pretend to wash hands and face*]
All by myself. [*point to self*]
I can put my toys and blocks in place [*pretend to put things away*]
All by myself. [*point to self*]

SUGGESTION: There are lots of details to act out as the class learns this verse. Have children practice the poem with a partner or small group. Different groups can act out each specific action.

The Alphabet Song

A – B – C – D – E – F – G,

H – I – J – K – L – M – N – O – P,

Q – R – S,

T – U – V,

W – X,

Y and Z.

Now I've said my ABCs.

Tell me what you think of me.

SUGGESTION: Almost all children know this song by the time they go to school. Encourage everyone to chime in with gusto.

fold
here

The Ants Go Marching

The ants go marching one by one,

Hurrah, hurrah.

The ants go marching one by one,

Hurrah, hurrah.

The ants go marching one by one,

The little one stops to suck his thumb.

And they all go marching down,

Into the ground,

To get out of the rain.

BOOM! BOOM! BOOM!

SUGGESTION: Have the children sing the song. Add new verses like the following: *two by two . . . tie his shoes | three by three .
. . climb a tree | four by four . . . shut the door | five by five . . . take a dive | six by six . . . pick up sticks | seven by seven . . . yell out
seven | eight by eight . . . shut the gate | nine by nine . . . check the time | ten by ten . . . say "The End!"*

Apple Harvest

Up in the green orchard,

There is a green tree,

The finest of pippins that ever you see.

The apples are ripe and ready to fall,

And Richard and Robin shall gather them all.

SUGGESTION: Discuss the words *orchard* and *pippins*. Substitute children's names for *Richard* and *Robin*.

Apples, Peaches

Apples, peaches,

Pears, plums,

Tell me when your

Birthday comes.

SUGGESTION: Help children learn the months of the year by reciting this rhyme: chant it repeatedly, followed by the name of each month of the year, in sequence. Have children raise their hands or stand up if their birthday occurs in the month that is said.

Are You Sleeping?

Are you sleeping, are you sleeping,

Brother John? Brother John?

Morning bells are ringing,

Morning bells are ringing,

Ding, ding, dong,

Ding, ding, dong.

FRENCH TRANSLATION:
Frère Jacques, Frère Jacques,
Dormez-vous? Dormez-vous?
Sonnez les matines,
Sonnez les matines,
Din, din, don,
Din, din, don.

SUGGESTION: Have child pretend to be asleep. Wake them up one at a time, inserting an appropriate name each time and speeding up the tempo. Let children ring bells or tap glasses containing different levels of water in order to provide the sound effects. Try this as a two- or three-part round, each successive group beginning to sing when the previous group has finished line two. The class might enjoy learning the French version also.

As I Was Going Along

As I was going along, along,

A-singing a comical song, song, song,

The lane that I went was so long, long, long,

And the song that I sang was so long, long, long,

And so I went singing along.

SUGGESTION: This is a good poem to sing or chant as children march around the room. Children may notice that every line has the same sound at the end—*song, long, along.*

As I Was Walking

As I was walking near the lake,

I met a little rattlesnake.

He ate so much jelly-cake,

It made his little belly ache.

SUGGESTION: Have the children rub their tummies at the end. You can change this poem by substituting colors or other adjectives *(yellow snake, slimy snake, wiggly snake).*

Baa, Baa, Black Sheep

Baa, baa, black sheep,

Have you any wool?

Yes sir, yes sir, three bags full.

One for the master,

And one for the dame,

And one for the little boy

Who lives down the lane.

VARIATION:
Moo, moo, brown cow,
Have you any milk?
Yes miss, three jugs smooth as silk.
One for you,
And one for me,
And one for the little cat
Who sits in the tree.

SUGGESTION: Teach everyone this rhyme, and then ask one group of children to say or sing the question, a second group to say or sing the response. Everyone may hold up one finger each time the word *one* is repeated. Help children come up with additional versions or variations of this rhyme, such as the one provided.

Baby Mice

Where are the baby mice?

Squeak, squeak, squeak.

I cannot see them.

Peek, peek, peek.

Here they come

From a hole in the wall,

One, two, three, four, five

In all!

SUGGESTION: Children enjoy pretending to be squeaking, peeking baby mice. (Masks, made from paper plates attached to tongue depressors, make it even more fun.) Have one half of the class be mice while the other half recites the poem. Then trade roles. Who is looking for these mice? A lost mouse, a child, a cat? There are many ways to interpret and share this nursery rhyme. Teach accompanying hand movements when the rhyme is familiar: hold one hand behind the back when looking for the mice, bring it forward (as a fist) when peeking, and uncurl one digit at a time when counting.

Baby Seeds

In a milkweed cradle, snug and warm,

Baby seeds are hiding safe from harm.

Open wide the cradle, hold it high,

Come along wind, help them fly.

ACTIONS:
In a milkweed cradle, snug and warm, [*close fingers into fist*]
Baby seeds are hiding safe from harm.
Open wide the cradle, hold it high, [*open hand and hold it up high*]
Come along wind, help them fly. [*wiggle fingers*]

SUGGESTION: Milkweed grows in only a few parts of the country, but if you can bring some in so children can see the "milkweed cradle," they will be fascinated. Many seeds fly on the wind—for example, dandelions. Look at some seeds together.

The Beach

White sand,

Sea sand,

Warm sand,

Kicking sand,

Building sand,

Watching sand

As the waves roll in.

SUGGESTION: This poem evokes visual images. Children might create other poems with descriptive words *(green grass)* or action words *(mowing grass)*.

fold
here

45

The Bear Went Over the Mountain

The bear went over the mountain,

The bear went over the mountain,

The bear went over the mountain,

To see what he could see.

And all that he could see,

And all that he could see,

Was the other side of the mountain,

The other side of the mountain,

The other side of the mountain,

The other side of the mountain,

Was all that he could see.

SUGGESTION: Have children sing this rhyme to the tune of "For He's a Jolly Good Fellow." It's lots of fun, especially while reading along with Rosemary Wells's picture book *The Bear Went Over the Mountain*. Children will enjoy making a simple mural and showing the "bear" (as stick puppet) going over the mountain.

Bedtime

Down with the lambs,

Up with the lark,

Run to bed, children,

Before it gets dark.

SUGGESTION: Help children understand the references to going to bed early *Down with the lambs* and getting up early *Up with the lark*. After they've learned the verse, have one group read the first line, a second group read the second line, and everyone read the last two lines.

Beets

I eat my beets with jelly;

I eat all afternoon.

It makes them really smelly,

But it keeps them on the spoon.

SUGGESTION: Children will enjoy inventing variations on this nonsense poem. *I eat my cereal [peas, broccoli, etc.] with jelly.* See another variation of this rhyme, "Peas," also in this volume.

Big and Small

I can make myself real big

By standing up straight and tall.

But when I'm tired of being big,

I can make myself get small.

SUGGESTION: Children can make themselves "big," "tall," and "small" as they recite this poem. They are learning "dance levels"—different ways to move in space.

Big Turkey

There was a big turkey on a steep green hill,

And he said, "Gobble, gobble, gobble, gobble."

His tail spread out like a big feather fan,

And he said, "Gobble, gobble, gobble, gobble."

SUGGESTION: After children learn the rhyme, they can have their own "Turkey Rhythm Band." Have them use tambourines, rhythm sticks, paper towel rolls, and spoons to accentuate the beat.

Billy, Billy

"Billy, Billy come and play,

While the sun shines bright as day."

"Yes, my friend, that's what I'll do,

Because I like to play with you."

ADDITIONAL VERSES
"Billy, Billy, have you seen
Sam and Betsy on the green?"
"Yes, my friend, I saw them pass,
Skipping over the nice cut grass."

"Billy, Billy, come along,
And I will sing a funny song."

SUGGESTION: Read this poem as question and answer. Substitute a child's name in the first line and have that child answer.

Bingo

There was a farmer who had a dog,

And Bingo was his name. Oh!

B – I – N – G – O,

B – I – N – G – O,

B – I – N – G – O,

And Bingo was his name. Oh!

VARIATION:
There was a cowboy rode a horse,
And Dusty was his name. Oh!
D – U – S – T – Y,
D – U – S – T – Y,
D – U – S – T – Y,
And Dusty was his name. Oh!

SUGGESTION: Sing this song once in its entirety. The second time through, leave off the *B*, substituting a clap, a finger snap, or other short sound. The next time through, clap (or whatever) for *B* and *I*. Continue until all five letters have been replaced with claps.

Blackberries

Blackberries, blackberries, on the hill.

How many pails can you fill?

Briers are thick and briers scratch,

But we'll pick all the berries

In the blackberry patch.

SUGGESTION: Have the children snap their fingers or clap on the rhyming words. You can substitute other fruits for blackberries.

fold
here

53

Blow, Wind, Blow

Blow, wind, blow! And go, mill, go!

That the miller can grind his corn,

That the baker can take it,

And into bread make it,

And bring us a loaf in the morn.

SUGGESTION: You many need to explain that a *miller* was a person who ground corn to make bread. Refer to the story of the Little Red Hen if they know it. Add simple sound effects for *blow* and *go*. Children will need support learning this archaic syntax.

Bouncing Ball

I'm bouncing, bouncing, everywhere,

I bounce and bounce into the air.

I'm bouncing, bouncing like a ball,

I bounce and bounce until I fall.

SUGGESTION: Bouncing is the ticket for enjoying these words. Invite children to bounce up and down as they say the rhyme and then drop to the floor.

Bow-Wow-Wow

Bow-wow-wow!

Whose dog art thou?

Little Tommy Tinker's dog,

Bow-wow-wow!

SUGGESTION: Have half the group play the dog, the other half the questioner. Children will need help with the archaic syntax of this poem but will enjoy fast repetition with a different child's name each time.

Cackle, Cackle, Mother Goose

Cackle, cackle, Mother Goose,

Have you any feathers loose?

Yes I have, my pretty fellow,

Just enough to fill a pillow.

SUGGESTION: Children may be unfamiliar with the word *cackle* and may need to discuss the fact that many pillows are filled with feathers. Assign one child to read the final two lines. If children are looking at the print, they may notice all the double letters in the words.

fold
here

The Candle

Little Nancy Etticoat

With a white petticoat,

And a red nose;

She has no feet or hands,

The longer she stands,

The shorter she grows.

SUGGESTION: This rhyme is really a riddle. And the title provides the answer. Teach the children the rhyme without giving them the title and see if they can answer it. You may want to draw a picture as they recite it to give them a visual clue.

The Cat

The cat sat asleep by the side of the fire.

The mistress snored loud as a pig.

Jack took up his fiddle by Jenny's desire,

And struck up a bit of a jig.

SUGGESTION: The snoring sound that can be added to the end of the second line will be very popular! Three different children (*cat, mistress,* and *Jack*) can act out the poem while the rest say the rhyme.

fold
here

59

Catch Him, Crow

Catch him, crow! Carry him, kite!

Take him away until the apples are ripe.

When they are ripe and ready to fall,

Here comes baby, apples and all.

SUGGESTION: What's that baby doing up there, anyway? This poem can lead to an interesting discussion. Once they understand what is going on in this verse, children love to shout, "Catch him, crow! Carry him, kite!" This is a good poem for children to illustrate.

Caterpillar

"Who's that tickling my back?"

Said the wall.

"Me," said a small caterpillar,

"I'm learning to crawl."

SUGGESTION: This poem has a surprise point of view: a wall asks the question, and the caterpillar answers. Have assigned children read the dialogue, or read the first two lines and ask children to think about what could be "tickling" a wall. The final two lines will confirm their predictions.

fold
here

61

Charlie Over the Ocean

Charlie over the ocean,

Charlie over the sea,

Charlie caught a blackbird,

But he can't catch me.

SUGGESTION: Who is Charlie? What is going on here? Children will have lots of ideas. Substitute other children's names.
Have children point to themselves at the end. Assign the first three lines to three smaller groups and have the whole
group read the last line.

Chickery, Chickery, Cranny, Crow

Chickery, chickery, cranny, crow,

Went to the well to wash my toe.

When I got back, my chicken was gone.

What will I do from dusk to dawn?

SUGGESTION: Ask children what they think is going on in this rhyme, and have them tell their own versions of the story. Invite the children to clap on the rhyming words, whisper them, or say them loudly.

fold here

63

Chocolate Rhyme

One, two, three, cho—

One, two, three, co—

One, two, three, la—

One, two, three, te!

Stir, stir the chocolate.

SUGGESTION: Have children count with their fingers and then mime stirring the chocolate. They can clap the word *chocolate* to identify syllable breaks or say the word slowly to identify sounds.

Clap Your Hands

Clap your hands, one, two, three.

Clap your hands just like me.

Wiggle your fingers, one, two, three.

Wiggle your fingers just like me.

SUGGESTION: Have the children clap their hands and wiggle their fingers as they say the rhyme. These movements strengthen children's hands and help them develop fine motor control, just as the words help them develop phonemic awareness and vocabulary. You can have children make up new motions as you go around in a circle (*Kick your foot, Rub your tummy, Nod your head*).

fold
here

Cobbler, Cobbler

Cobbler, cobbler, mend my shoe,

Get it done by half past two;

Stitch it up and stitch it down,

Then I'll give you half a crown.

SUGGESTION: Children are intrigued when they find out that a *crown* is an old-time coin, not just a special headdress worn by a king or queen. Pair this verse with the classic tale *The Elves and the Shoemaker* by the Brothers Grimm.

Color Song

Red is the color for an apple to eat.

Red is the color for cherries, too.

Red is the color for strawberries.

I like red, don't you?

ADDITIONAL VERSES:

Blue is the color for the big blue sky.
Blue is the color for baby things, too.
Blue is the color of my sister's eyes.
I like blue, don't you?

Yellow is the color for the great big sun.
Yellow is the color for lemonade, too.
Yellow is the color of a baby chick.
I like yellow, don't you?

Green is the color for the leaves on the trees.
Green is the color for green peas, too.
Green is the color of a watermelon.
I like green, don't you?

Orange is the color for oranges that grow.
Orange is the color for carrots, too.
Orange is the color of a pumpkin.
I like orange, don't you?

SUGGESTION: Using the same structure, create new verses for other colors, such as *black, brown, gray, pink, purple.*

fold
here

67

Come and Listen

Come and listen,

Come and listen,

To my song,

To my song.

Happy children singing,

Happy children singing,

Sing along,

Sing along.

SUGGESTION: This rhyme can be sung to the tune of "Are You Sleeping?" It's a good one to use as the class gathers for various activities.

Come, Butter, Come

Come, butter, come,

Come, butter, come.

_____'s at the garden gate,

Waiting with banana cake.

Come, butter, come.

SUGGESTION: Children probably won't know a lot about making butter. As they learn this poem, have them sit in a circle and pass around a tub of whipping cream. Have each child shake the container and hand it to the next person. Very shortly the liquid will start to thicken. It won't be long before children notice that the liquid in the tub has stopped swishing around and now thumps and clunks. The liquid has become a solid and they have made butter! Spread the butter on crackers and eat them together.

Cross Patch

Cross patch, draw the latch,

Sit by the fire and spin.

Take a cup and drink it up,

And let your neighbors in.

SUGGESTION: To the beat, have pairs of children perform the following sequence twice, once on the first two lines, again on the last two lines: clap thighs, clap hands, clap partner's palms face front, clap hands, clap thighs, clap hands, and clap partner's palms face front.

Cuckoo, Cuckoo

Cuckoo, cuckoo, cherry tree,

Cuckoo, cuckoo, cherry tree.

Catch a bird and give it to me.

Let the tree be high or low,

Sunshine, wind, or rain, or snow.

SUGGESTION: Explain that a *cuckoo* is a kind of bird. Children will enjoy the contrast in this poem (*high* and *low*) as well as the weather words.

fold here

Dance a Merry Jig

This little pig danced a merry, merry jig.

This little pig ate candy.

This little pig wore a blue and yellow wig.

This little pig was a dandy.

But this little pig never grew very big,

And they called her itty bitty Mandy.

SUGGESTION: Have the children touch their fingers as they say the rhyme. Because there are so many specific details in this rhyme, it's a great one to use for directed drawing: see how many of the things mentioned in the poem children will include in their artwork as you read and reread the poem. In subsequent readings of the poem, substitute other names that rhyme with *Mandy* (*Andy, Sandy, Randy*).

Dickory, Dickory, Dare!

Dickory, dickory, dare!

The pig flew up in the air;

The man in brown,

Soon brought him down.

Dickory, dickory, dare!

SUGGESTION: Introduce this variation after the more familiar verse *Hickory, Dickory, Dock* along with another version *Hickory Dickory, Dore* (both included in this book). Children will love to compare the variations and perhaps recite them in a "Hickory, Dickory" performance. Three groups could each rehearse a variation and perform it for the other groups. Be sure to point out how the title and text change when substituting *d* for *h* in the word *Hickory*. This is a good example to use when working with hearing and substituting sounds.

fold here

Did You Ever See a Lassie?

Did you ever see a lassie, a lassie, a lassie?

Did you ever see a lassie

Go this way and that?

Go this way and that way,

And this way and that way?

Did you ever see a lassie go this way and that?

SUGGESTION: Teach children the tune by singing or playing the song yourself or by playing a recording of it. Have groups of children sing this song as a question-and-answer exchange: "Did you ever . . . ? No, I never . . ." Substitute *laddie* for *lassie*. Expand the vocabulary by seeing what other things children want to ask: *Did you ever see a space ship? Did you ever see an elephant?* and so on. Write down children's responses and read them back together. Compile these responses in a class book.

Diddle, Diddle, Dumpling

Diddle, diddle, dumpling, my son John,

Went to bed with his breeches on.

One shoe off and one shoe on,

Diddle, diddle, dumpling, my son John.

SUGGESTION: Talk about the word *breeches* (meaning *pants*) and substitute other crazy things you could wear to bed. Children love coming up with ideas, from swimsuits to bike helmets. Substitute other names as well.

fold
here

75

Diddlety, Diddlety, Dumpty

Diddlety, diddlety, dumpty,

The cat ran up the plum tree;

Half a crown to fetch her down,

Diddlety, diddlety, dumpty.

SUGGESTION: Point out that a *crown* is an old-time coin. Children may want to substitute *half-dollar*. They may notice that *diddlety* and *dumpty* have endings that sound alike. Have them say these words slowly and listen for the sound.

A Diller, A Dollar

A diller, a dollar,

A ten o'clock scholar,

What makes you come so soon?

You used to come at ten o'clock,

But now you come at noon.

SUGGESTION: Children may not be familiar with the word *scholar,* so be sure to talk about that with them. Also, let children puzzle over whether noon is sooner or later than ten o'clock. Use a clock with movable hands to show the different times mentioned in the poem.

fold
here

77

Doodlebug

Doodlebug, doodlebug, come get sweet milk.

Doodlebug, doodlebug, come get some butter.

Doodlebug, doodlebug, come get corn bread.

Doodlebug, doodlebug, come get supper.

SUGGESTION: Add some sound effects made with an instrument such as a xylophone or a tambourine to accompany *doodlebug* each time it is read. Since the poem does not rhyme, it's easy to increase it to include many favorite foods.

Dormy, Dormy, Dormouse

Dormy, dormy, dormouse,

Sleeps in his little house.

He won't wake up until suppertime,

And that won't be until half past nine.

SUGGESTION: Have children imagine a small animal that looks like a mouse and is very sleepy. Point out how *dormy* and *dormouse* start alike and how *house* and *mouse* rhyme.

Down by the Station

Down by the station,

Early in the morning,

See the little puffer-bellies,

All in a row.

See the engine driver,

Pull the little throttle.

Puff, puff! Toot, toot!

Off we go.

SUGGESTION: Simple instruments, such as a bell and a tambourine, can be used to emphasize the words *puff* and *toot*.
Children will enjoy scooting around the room to make a "train." You can also have children sit in a line to read the poem,
reaching and pulling their right arms for *Puff, puff!* and their left arms for *Toot, toot!*

Downy Duck

One day I saw a downy duck

With feathers on his back.

I said, "Good morning, downy duck."

And he said, "Quack, quack, quack."

SUGGESTION: A little duck puppet (with feathers on his back) is perfect for children to use to act out this poem. If you can't find a downy duck puppet, have children draw pictures of a duck, cut them out, and attach them to their index fingers using strips of construction paper glued to form a cylinder. Assign a child to read each of the dialogue parts.

fold here

The Elephant Goes Like This

The elephant goes like this, like that.

He's terribly big,

And he's terribly fat,

He has no fingers,

He has no toes,

But goodness gracious,

What a nose!

ACTIONS:
The elephant goes like this, like that. [*move on all fours, slowly like an elephant*]
He's terribly big, [*stand up and reach arms high*]
And he's terribly fat, [*stretch arms out to the sides*]
He has no fingers, [*make a fist and hide fingers*]
He has no toes, [*wiggle toes*]
But goodness gracious,
What a nose! [*point to nose*]

SUGGESTION: Have a whole line of children troop through the classroom, swinging their trunks and swaying. Recite the poem together in slow "elephant" rhythm, adding the motions.

Elizabeth, Elspeth, Betsey, and Bess

Elizabeth, Elspeth, Betsey, and Bess,

They all went together to seek a hen's nest;

They found a hen's nest with five eggs in,

They all took an egg, and left one in.

SUGGESTION: Substitute the names of four children in the class. Cut out representations of the characters, a hen's nest, and five eggs and affix them to small magnets; then have children retell the story as they manipulate the cutouts on a magnetic cookie sheet or whiteboard.

fold
here

83

Elsie Marley

Elsie Marley's grown so fine,

She won't get up to feed the swine,

But lies in bed until eight or nine!

Lazy Elsie Marley.

SUGGESTION: Substitute children's names or nonsense two-part names for *Elsie Marley*. Children may not know that *swine* is another name for *pig* or that sleeping until eight or nine o'clock would mean sleeping past the start of school.

Every Morning at Eight O'Clock

Every morning at eight o'clock,

You can hear the mail carrier's knock.

Up jumps Katy to open the door,

One letter, two letters, three letters, four.

SUGGESTION: This poem is ideal for children to act out. You can prepare letter cards that spell children's names or high frequency words. The child named in the poem ("Katy") can deliver the letters.

fold
here

The Farmer in the Dell

The farmer in the dell,

The farmer in the dell,

Hi-ho, the derry-o,

The farmer in the dell.

ADDITIONAL VERSES:
The farmer takes a wife . . .
The wife takes a child . . .
The child takes a nurse . . .
The nurse takes a cow . . .
The cow takes a dog . . .
The dog takes a cat . . .
The cat takes a rat . . .
The rat takes the cheese . . .
The cheese stands alone . . .

fold
here

SUGGESTION: Have the children join hands and form a circle around one child chosen as the farmer. As they sing, every-one walks in one direction. At the end of each verse, the chosen "character" chooses the next one to join them in the middle. To continue until everyone has been chosen may require repeating the song as the "cheese" child, standing alone, becomes the new farmer.

Father, Mother, and Uncle John

Father, Mother, and Uncle John

Went to market one by one.

Father fell off,

Mother fell off,

But Uncle John rode on and on.

And on,

And on,

And on,

And on,

And on . . .

SUGGESTION: Substitute children's names for *Uncle John*. What kinds of things might these characters ride to the market? Cars, dragons, horses, donkeys? You will develop vocabulary as the children list all their ideas. Read the ideas back as a group. Which ones do the children think are logical?

fold here

Fiddle-de-dee

Fiddle-de-dee, fiddle-de-dee,

The fly shall marry the bumblebee.

They went to the hall, and married was she,

The fly has married the bumblebee.

SUGGESTION: Children will need practice to master the unusual syntax of this poem, but it will increase their awareness of the structure of written language. If children are looking at the poem, point out the double *ee* in words.

Fido

I have a little dog

And his name is Fido.

He is nothing but a pup.

He can stand on his hind legs

If you hold his front legs up.

SUGGESTION: Substitute the names of the pet dogs of children in your class (or other names the children may suggest).
Place children's dog drawings around the printed poem on a poetry chart. Ask children to say *up* and *pup* and listen for the
ending sound.

fold
here

89

Five Fat Peas

Five fat peas in a peapod pressed,

One grew, two grew, and so did the rest.

They grew and grew and did not stop,

Until one day the pod went POP!

SUGGESTION: Children love this infectious counting rhyme and the images of peas growing and the pea pod popping. Invite your class to clap when the pod "pops"! Have children sing it to the tune of "Twinkle, Twinkle, Little Star."

Five Fat Pumpkins

Five fat pumpkins sitting on a gate.

First one said, "Oh my, it's getting late."

Second one said, "There's a bat in the air."

Third one said, "We don't care."

Fourth one said, "Let's run, run, run."

Fifth one said, "Let's have some fun."

But whooo went the wind and out went the light

And five fat pumpkins rolled out of sight.

SUGGESTION: This rhyme can be done as a finger play: hold up five fingers, wiggle one for each quote, cup mouth and blow for the wind, and roll one hand over the other during the last line. Or, five pumpkins can sit on a "gate" and mime the actions of the poem as the rest of the class recites the words. Secretly tell one child to turn off the classroom lights on the words "out went the light." Children also love making pumpkin puppets from cut paper and kraft sticks.

Five Fingers on Each Hand

I have five fingers on each hand,

Ten toes on my two feet,

Two ears, two eyes,

One nose, one mouth,

With which to sweetly speak.

My hands can clap, my feet can tap,

My eyes can clearly see,

My ears can hear,

My nose can sniff,

My mouth can say, "I'm me."

SUGGESTION: Have the children indicate the appropriate body parts. You can use Lois Ehlert's picture book *Hands* with this rhyme as well. Have children trace their hands on construction paper and cut them out.

Five Little Ducks

Five little ducks went out one day,

Over the hills and far away,

Mother Duck said, "Quack, quack, quack, quack,"

But only four little ducks came back.

SUGGESTION: After children have learned this verse and are familiar with the words, you can use it as a countdown poem. Revisit this when you are working with number words. The last line changes during the "one little duck" verse: *And all the five little ducks came back.*

Five Little Ducks Went in for a Swim

Five little ducks went in for a swim.

The first little duck put his head in.

The second little duck put his head back.

The third little duck said, "Quack, quack, quack."

The fourth little duck with his tiny brother

Went for a walk with his father and mother.

ACTIONS:

Five little ducks went in for a swim. [*wiggle fingers*]

The first little duck put his head in. [*put head forward*]

The second little duck put his head back. [*put head back*]

The third little duck said, "Quack, quack, quack." [*clap three times*]

The fourth little duck with his tiny brother

Went for a walk with his father and mother. [*walk fingers*]

fold
here

SUGGESTION: Perform a little duck finger play.

Five Little Fingers

One little finger standing on its own.

Two little fingers, now they're not alone.

Three little fingers happy as can be.

Four little fingers go walking down the street.

Five little fingers, this one is a thumb.

Wave bye-bye because now we are done.

ACTIONS:
One little finger standing on its own. [*hold up index finger*]
Two little fingers, now they're not alone. [*add middle finger*]
Three little fingers happy as can be. [*add ring finger*]
Four little fingers go walking down the street. [*add little finger and wiggle all four fingers*]
Five little fingers, this one is a thumb. [*add the thumb*]
Wave bye-bye because now we are done. [*wave good-bye*]

SUGGESTION: Teach the children the finger actions to go along with the rhyme. As a follow-up, share Lois Ehlert's picture book *Hands*, which has a cardboard cover shaped like a work glove. The book shows all kinds of things hands can do.

fold here

Five Little Froggies

Five little froggies sitting on a well,

One looked up and down she fell.

Froggies jumped high,

Froggies jumped low,

Four little froggies dancing to and fro.

SUGGESTION: Children will clamber to be froggies: jumping high and low and dancing to and fro as they act out the poem. The rest of the group can recite the poem. This poem can also be used as a countdown poem once children are familiar with the verse. It can be turned into a feltboard or magnet board poem, with children removing a frog with each verse.

Five Little Monkeys in a Tree

Five little monkeys

Swinging in a tree,

Teasing Mr. Crocodile,

"You can't catch me!"

Along comes Mr. Crocodile,

Quiet as can be.

Snap!

Four little monkeys

Swinging in a tree.

SUGGESTION: Children love to act out this rhyme. The most popular character is the crocodile, who gets to "snap." Have the children continue the rhyme, substituting the appropriate numbers, until all the monkeys have been snapped up by the crocodile.

Five Little Monkeys on the Bed

Five little monkeys jumping on the bed,

One fell off and bumped his head.

Mama called the doctor, and the doctor said,

"No more monkeys jumping on the bed!"

SUGGESTION: Children will enjoy acting out this poem: you need five monkeys, the doctor, and Mama. Continue the countdown, having one monkey leave the circle each time. Substitute another animal for a variation.

Five Little Sausages

Five little sausages frying in a pan,

Sizzle, sizzle, sizzle, and one went BAM!

Four little sausages frying in a pan,

Sizzle, sizzle, sizzle, and one went BAM!

Three little sausages frying in a pan,

Sizzle, sizzle, sizzle, and one went BAM!

Two little sausages frying in a pan,

Sizzle, sizzle, sizzle, and one went BAM!

One little sausage frying in a pan,

Sizzle, sizzle, sizzle, and it went BAM!

SUGGESTION: Children enjoy shouting *BAM!* at the end of each verse and may clap spontaneously when they do so. You can also ask them to emphasize the *s* and *z* sounds of *sizzle* to suggest how these sausages sound when they cook. Have them hold up and wiggle five fingers on the first verse, one less on each successive verse.

Five Little Snowmen

Five little snowmen happy and gay,

The first one said, "What a nice day!"

The second one said, "We'll cry no tears."

The third one said, "We'll stay for years."

The fourth one said, "But what happens in May?"

The fifth one said, "Look, we're melting away!"

SUGGESTION: As children learn the rhyme, have them hold up one hand and wiggle a digit during each snowman quote, increasing one digit with each line. At the end they can hold out a closed fist to indicate that all the snowmen are gone. Once they have learned the words, assign five children to read the quoted lines while the rest of the children serve as narrators, reciting (in unison) the first line and the beginning of each successive line.

A Frog Sat on a Log

A frog sat on a log,

A-weeping for his daughter.

His eyes were red,

His tears he shed,

And he fell right into the water.

SUGGESTION: Invite the children to imagine what happened to Frog's daughter and why he is crying. Have children identify words in the rhyme that have the same ending sound.

fold here

101

Frosty Weather

Frosty weather,

Snowy weather,

When the wind blows,

We all go together.

SUGGESTION: Invite the children to imagine the sound of the wind. Ask some to supply "wind sounds" as the other children say the verse. They can also generate other words that go with *frosty* and *snowy*.

Fuzzy Wuzzy

Fuzzy Wuzzy was a bear.

Fuzzy Wuzzy had no hair.

Fuzzy Wuzzy wasn't fuzzy,

Was he?

SUGGESTION: After children learn the poem and can say the words, they can discuss what Fuzzy Wuzzy looks like. Help children notice the subtle pronunciation difference between *wuzzy* and *was he*, as well as attend to the rising tone signaled by the question mark.

Georgy Porgy

Georgy Porgy, pudding and pie,

Kissed the girls and made them cry.

When the boys came out to play,

Georgy Porgy ran away.

SUGGESTION: Have children clap twice on Georgy and twice on Porgy as they read or recite the rhyme.

Giddyup

Giddyup, giddyup,

One, two, three.

Giddyup, giddyup,

Come see me.

SUGGESTION: Have children take turns reading specific lines. Extend the rhyme by writing it on chart paper (or a pocket chart), inserting "Four, five, six" and asking children if they can think of a rhyming line. Children easily figure out what actions go with *giddyup* and enjoy pretending to ride.

fold here

105

Go In and Out the Window

Go in and out the window,

Go in and out the window,

Go in and out the window,

As we have done before.

SUGGESTION: This is a game song. Have children form a circle and raise clasped hands. The child who is "it" chooses a partner and grabs on at the waist. They go in and out the "windows" formed by the raised arms, then the chosen partner chooses another partner.

Go to Bed

Go to bed late,

Stay very small.

Go to bed early,

Grow very tall.

SUGGESTION: Many rhymes recommend beneficial behavior. Discuss the importance of getting enough sleep. Ask children what helps them go to sleep at night. Teddy bears? Special blankets? Being told a bedtime story or sung a lullaby? Saying a poem or retelling a story in their head? Have children recite the rhyme together, crouching on the word *small* and stretching up high when they say *tall*.

Go to Bed Early

Go to bed early—wake up with joy,

Go to bed late—tired girl or boy;

Go to bed early—ready for play,

Go to bed late—moping all day;

Go to bed early—no pains or ills,

Go to bed late—doctors and pills;

Go to bed early—grow very tall,

Go to bed late—stay very small.

SUGGESTION: This is an old instruction rhyme showing the importance of a good night's sleep. After children are familiar with the words, have them create their own actions to accompany each line: how well can they improvise? Or have two groups alternate reading the lines.

Gobble, Gobble, Gobble

Gobble, gobble, gobble,

Quack, quack, quack,

A turkey says gobble,

And a duck says quack.

SUGGESTION: Have different children take turns gobbling, quacking, and reading this verse. Help them create new verses: ask them to suggest other animals and the sounds they make; then arrange the words into this same pattern. Ask them to clap the syllables of the animal sounds in each line to see if their suggestions will match. (*Meow, meow, meow; bow-wow-wow; oink, oink, oink; moo, moo, moo* are some animal noises that can be substituted.)

fold here

Good Morning

Good morning,

Good morning,

How are you?

How are you?

Very well, I thank you,

Very well, I thank you,

How about you?

How about you?

ADDITIONAL VERSES:

Good afternoon,
Good afternoon,
How are you?
How are you?
Very well, I thank you,
Very well, I thank you,
How about you?
How about you?

Good evening,
Good evening,
How are you?
How are you?
Very well, I thank you,
Very well, I thank you,
How about you?
How about you?

SUGGESTION: This "piggyback song" can be sung to the tune of "Are You Sleeping?" Introduce the poem in the morning using the first verse and revisit with the other verses at appropriate times of day. Children may create wilder and more imaginative words to the tune.

Good Morning to You

Good morning to you!

Good morning to you!

We're all in our places

With bright shining faces.

Oh, this is the way to start a great day!

ADDITIONAL VERSES:

Good noontime to you!
Good noontime to you!
We're all feeling yummy
With food in our tummy.
Oh, this is the way to have a great day!

A good-bye to you!
A good-bye to you!
We'll leave as the day ends
And go home to see friends.
Oh, this is the way to end a great day!

SUGGESTION: This old song has some new verses, and children may want to create more. Teach this song one verse at a time at the appropriate time of day. It then becomes a good gathering verse when children arrive in the morning, return from lunch, and line up to leave.

Grandpa Grig

Grandpa Grig

Had a pig

In a field of clover;

Piggy died,

Grandpa cried,

And all the fun was over.

SUGGESTION: Create new verses with different names for grandpa that rhyme with other animal names, such as *Grandpa Bog / Had a dog*.

Gray Squirrel

Gray squirrel, gray squirrel,

Swish your bushy tail.

Wrinkle up your funny nose,

Hold an acorn in your toes.

Gray squirrel, gray squirrel,

Swish your bushy tail.

ACTIONS:
Gray squirrel, gray squirrel, [*stand with hands on bent knees*]
Swish your bushy tail. [*wiggle the behind*]
Wrinkle up your funny nose, [*wrinkle nose*]
Hold an acorn in your toes. [*pinch index finger and thumb together*]
Gray squirrel, gray squirrel, [*stand with hands on bent knees*]
Swish your bushy tail. [*wiggle the behind*]

SUGGESTION: Children enjoy performing the actions that accompany this rhyme. They also enjoy making hand puppets—drawing gray squirrels, cutting them out, and attaching them to kraft sticks.

fold
here

Great A

Great A, little a, bouncing B,

The cat's in the cupboard

And can't see me.

SUGGESTION: Select other upper- and lowercase letters to insert into the form. You can change *great* to *big* or use the words *uppercase* and *lowercase*. Children can hold up large letter cards at appropriate points in the poem.

Head, Shoulders, Knees, and Toes

Head, shoulders, knees, and toes,

Knees and toes.

Head, shoulders, knees, and toes,

Knees and toes.

And eyes and ears and mouth and nose.

Head, shoulders, knees, and toes,

Knees and toes.

SUGGESTION: Sing the song in its entirety, having the children touch their head, their shoulders, their knees, their toes, their eyes, their ears, their mouths, and their noses. The second time through, omit the word *head* but still perform the motion. Then omit *shoulders, knees, toes, eyes, ears, mouth,* and *nose* one at time, still performing the motions and going faster and faster.

Hear the Lively Song

Hear the lively song

Of the frogs in yonder pond.

Crick, crick, crickety-crick,

Burr-ump!

SUGGESTION: After children know this verse, it's fun to orchestrate the whole poem with four groups of children: frogs in the pond here, poetry narrators there, a place for the group saying *crick, crick, crickety-crick* and snapping their fingers, and one last little group providing the sound *Burr-ump!* This will be a spirited performance and will help make clear such words as *lively* and *yonder!*

Here Are My Ears

Here are my ears.
Here is my nose.
Here are my fingers.
Here are my toes.

Here are my eyes
Both open wide.
Here is my mouth
With white teeth inside.

Here is my tongue
That helps me speak.
Here is my chin
And here are my cheeks.

Here are my hands
That help me play.
Here are my feet
For walking today.

SUGGESTION: Have children point to or display each body part as they go through all the verses. English-language learn-ers especially benefit from identifying the body parts as they say the specific vocabulary. As an extension, have children draw a self-portrait and label the various bodily features. (You may want to work through the poem on chart paper and highlight or underline each body part so that children have a model for writing the words.)

Here Are My Eyes

Here are my eyes,

One and two.

I can wink.

So can you.

When my eyes are open,

I see the light.

When they are closed,

It's dark as night.

ACTIONS:

Here are my eyes, [*point to both eyes using two fingers*]
One and two. [*point to one eye at a time*]
I can wink. [*wink while pointing to self*]
So can you. [*wink while pointing to others*]

When my eyes are open, [*open eyes wide*]
I see the light.
When they are closed, [*close eyes*]
It's dark as night.

SUGGESTION: The simple actions suggested for this poem give children a little exercise for their eyes. Ask children to show how they "wink." This is a good poem for children to recite with partners after they are familiar with the words: they face each other and take turns saying the first verse (emphasizing *me* and *you*); then, in unison, they recite the second verse.

Here Is a Bunny

Here is a bunny with ears so funny,

And here is his hole in the ground.

When a noise he hears, he pricks up his ears,

And hops into his hole so round.

ACTIONS:
Here is a bunny with ears so funny, [*curl fingers over thumb and "bounce" two fingers*]
And here is his hole in the ground. [*make hole with thumb and forefinger of other hand*]
When a noise he hears, he pricks up his ears, [*hold "ears" up straight*]
And hops into his hole so round. [*hop bunny over into the "hole"*]

SUGGESTION: Children love performing this finger play. Make sure they know the words before they focus on the hand movements. To add interest, freeze and unfreeze the action from time to time with a tap from your magic wand (a pencil with a star attached).

Here Is a House

Here is a house built up high,

With two tall chimneys reaching the sky.

Here are the windows.

Here is the door.

If we peep inside

We'll see a mouse on the floor.

ACTIONS:

Here is a house built up high, [*stretch arms up, touching fingertips together like a roof*]

With two tall chimneys reaching the sky. [*stretch arms up separately*]

Here are the windows. [*make a square shape with hands*]

Here is the door. [*pantomime knocking*]

If we peep inside [*tilt head as if looking around a corner*]

We'll see a mouse on the floor. [*move fingers like a running mouse*]

SUGGESTION: Have children act out the rhyme. As an alternative, create a simple drawing of a big house with appropriate features and a door that opens, showing a mouse. Children can point to parts of the house, opening the door at the end.

Here Is the Sea

Here is the sea,

The wavy sea,

Here is a boat,

And here is me.

And all the fishes

Down below

Wiggle their tails

And away they go.

ACTIONS:
Here is the sea, [*wave hands from side to side*]
The wavy sea, [*wiggle fingers*]
Here is a boat, [*cup hands like a boat*]
And here is me. [*point to yourself*]

And all the fishes [*wiggle fingers*]
Down below [*point down*]
Wiggle their tails [*wiggle fingers*]
And away they go. [*wiggle fingers behind back*]

SUGGESTION: Children love making motions for each line of this verse to indicate "the wavy sea," "the boat," "me," and especially the "fishes" who "wiggle their tails" and swim away. Children may enjoy working with a partner.

fold
here

121

Here We Go

Here we go—up, up, up.

Here we go—down, down, down.

Here we go—moving forward.

Here we go—moving backward.

Here we go—round and round and round.

ACTIONS:

Here we go—up, up, up. [*stand up on toes*]

Here we go—down, down, down. [*crouch down low*]

Here we go—moving forward. [*take a step forward*]

Here we go—moving backward. [*take a step backward*]

Here we go—round and round and round. [*spin*]

SUGGESTION: Children need frequent opportunities to move around as they vocalize. They will enjoy this stretch-and-transition rhyme. The natural movements appropriate for each line get children active while helping them remember the sequence of the words. Talk with children about words in the poem that are *opposites;* the actions will help them understand this concept.

Hey Diddle Diddle

Hey diddle diddle, the cat and the fiddle,

The cow jumped over the moon;

The little dog laughed to see such sport,

And the dish ran away with the spoon.

SUGGESTION: Create new verses by substituting different one-syllable animal names in place of *cow*. Invite children to draw and cut out elements of the poem (cat, fiddle, cow, moon, dog, dish, and spoon). They can glue the pieces on paper to create a scene.

fold
here

123

Hiccup, Hiccup

Hiccup, hiccup, go away!

Come again another day.

Hiccup, hiccup, when I bake,

I will give you a butter-cake.

SUGGESTION: After children have learned this poem, assign roles: have one child say the words *hiccup, hiccup* (or pretend to hiccup and make the sound) while one group of children says the rest of the words and another group marks the beat with rhythm instruments. They can also substitute words for *butter*.

Hickety, Pickety

Hickety, pickety, my black hen.

She lays eggs for gentlemen.

Sometimes nine,

And sometimes ten.

Hickety, pickety, my black hen.

SUGGESTION: Children can use rhythm sticks or two paper towel tubes to tap out the rhythm of this poem. Once the poem is learned, select and have children tap one-, two-, and three-syllable words from the rhyme.

fold
here

125

Hickory, Dickory, Dock!

Hickory, dickory, dock!

The mouse ran up the clock;

The clock struck one,

The mouse did run.

Hickory, dickory, dock!

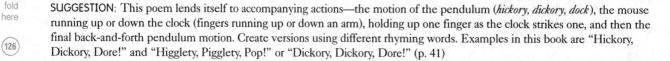

SUGGESTION: This poem lends itself to accompanying actions—the motion of the pendulum (*hickory, dickory, dock*), the mouse running up or down the clock (fingers running up or down an arm), holding up one finger as the clock strikes one, and then the final back-and-forth pendulum motion. Create versions using different rhyming words. Examples in this book are "Hickory, Dickory, Dore!" and "Higglety, Pigglety, Pop!" or "Dickory, Dickory, Dore!" (p. 41)

Hickory, Dickory, Dore!

Hickory, dickory, dore!

The dog sat on the floor;

The clock struck six,

The dog chewed sticks.

Hickory, dickory, dore!

SUGGESTION: Children will enjoy comparing this variation to the previous poem, "Hickory, Dickory, Dock." Another variation of this appears in the book, look for "Higglety, Pigglety, Pop!" Groups of children could each prepare a variation for presentation to the rest of the class.

fold
here

127

Higglety, Pigglety, Pop!

Higglety, pigglety, pop!

The dog has eaten the mop;

The pig's in a hurry,

The cat's in a flurry.

Higglety, pigglety, pop!

SUGGESTION: Children will enjoy making mental pictures of the messy activity described. Add sounds made on simple instruments (rhythm sticks, bells, or a tambourine) to highlight the words *Higglety, pigglety, pop!* Create new versions such as *Higglety, pigglety, peen! / The dog has eaten the screen*.

High and Low

I reach my hands way up high,

I can almost touch the sky.

Then I bend way down low,

And touch the floor just so.

SUGGESTION: This verse has the side benefit of some accompanying exercise, so it's a good transition activity. As you teach the poem to the children, add the movements called for by each line: reach hands high, stand on tiptoes, bend low, and touch the floor.

fold
here

129

Hippity Hop

Hippity hop to the candy shop

To buy a stick of candy.

One for you and one for me,

And one for sister Mandy.

SUGGESTION: The strong rhythm in this rhyme makes everyone want to "hippity hop" and act out the poem. have children say and clap the rhyming words (*candy, Mandy*) and think of others (*Andy, Sandy, Dandy*).

Hokey Pokey

You put your right hand in,

You put your right hand out,

You put your right hand in,

And you shake it all about.

You do the Hokey Pokey

And you turn yourself around,

That's what it's all about.

SUGGESTION: This is a lively break from the day's routine. It adds to the fun to play a recorded version of the song, if you have it, as children form a circle, put their left hand (or other specified body part) into and out of the circle, and then shake it. On the line *You do the Hokey Pokey*, have them raise both arms and wiggle their fingers as they turn around.

fold
here

131

Hot Cross Buns

Hot cross buns! Hot cross buns!

One-a-penny, two-a-penny,

Hot cross buns!

If you have no daughters,

Give them to your sons,

One-a-penny, two-a-penny,

Hot cross buns!

SUGGESTION: Explain that hot cross buns are bread rolls that have white icing "crosses" on them. They will enjoy clapping three times every time they say *Hot cross buns!*

How Many Days?

How many days do we have to play?

Saturday, Sunday, Monday—

Tuesday, Wednesday, Thursday,

Friday, Saturday, Sunday.

SUGGESTION: This poem helps children learn the days of the week. Create a slightly different verse by repeating the words of line one and then beginning line two with a different day. Since days of the week are always in the same order, starting with a new day changes the whole poem. Have children take turns picking a new day with which to begin. They can clap as they say each day. If children are looking at the poem, they can count the days.

Humpty Dumpty

Humpty Dumpty sat on a wall,

Humpty Dumpty had a great fall;

All the king's horses and all the king's men

Couldn't put Humpty together again.

SUGGESTION: Children may recite this poem in groups, one group saying the first two lines, the other group, the last two. You may want to create a feltboard version so that children can move Humpty Dumpty as they say the poem.

I Can Do It Myself

Hat on head, just like this,

Pull it down, you see.

I can put my hat on

By myself, just me.

ADDITIONAL VERSES:

One arm in, two arms in,
Buttons, one, two, three.
I can put my coat on
By myself, just me.

Toes in first, heels down next,
Pull and pull, then see—
I can put my boots on
By myself, just me.

Fingers here, thumbs right here,
Hands warm as can be.
I can put my mittens on
By myself, just me.

SUGGESTION: Perform this poem as a play, a different child acting out each verse using actual clothing (or just pantomiming putting on the garments). Make a shared-writing list of all the things children can do by themselves, and invite them to illustrate it.

I Clap My Hands

I clap my hands,

I touch my feet,

I jump up from the ground.

I clap my hands,

I touch my feet,

And turn myself around.

SUGGESTION: Have children perform the actions of the poem as they repeat it two or three times. Later, have them look at a printed version of the poem and pick out simple words such as *I* and *my*.

I Clap My Hands to Make a Sound

I clap my hands to make a sound—

Clap, clap, clap!

I tap my toes to make a sound—

Tap, tap, tap!

I open my mouth to say a word—

Talk, talk, talk!

I pick up my foot to take a step—

Walk, walk, walk!

SUGGESTION: Have children clap, tap, talk, and walk as they say this poem. Some of the class can be the audience while other children perform. Then reverse roles.

I Had a Loose Tooth

I had a loose tooth,
A wiggly, jiggly loose tooth.
I had a loose tooth,
A-hanging by a thread.

I pulled my loose tooth,
My wiggly, jiggly loose tooth.
Put it under my pillow,
And then I went to bed.

The fairy took my loose tooth,
My wiggly, jiggly loose tooth.
And now I have a quarter,
And a hole in my head.

ACTIONS:
I had a loose tooth,
A wiggly, jiggly loose tooth. [*pretend to wiggle a tooth as if it were in the mouth*]
I had a loose tooth,
A-hanging by a thread. [*hold hand up as if holding a tooth on a string*]

I pulled my loose tooth, [*pretend to pull tooth*]
My wiggly, jiggly loose tooth. [*pretend to shake tooth in palm of hand*]
Put it under my pillow,
And then I went to bed. [*put two hands together and lean head on them*]

The fairy took my loose tooth, [*pretend to hold up tooth*]
My wiggly, jiggly loose tooth. [*pretend to shake tooth in palm of hand*]
And now I have a quarter, [*hold palm out*]
And a hole in my head. [*point to jaw*]

SUGGESTION: Losing a tooth is a big event in a primary classroom. Children are compelled to talk about the experience and to demonstrate how the tooth finally fell out. Revisit this poem, and the accompanying actions (see above), each time a child looses a tooth. If you are using a printed version, children may notice the words with *-oo* spelling.

I Have a Little Wagon

I have a little wagon,

It goes all around the town.

I can pull it,

I can push it,

I can turn it upside down.

ACTIONS:
I have a little wagon, [*hold hand out, palm up*]
It goes all around the town. [*move hand around*]
I can pull it, [*pull hand in*]
I can push it, [*push hand away*]
I can turn it upside down. [*turn hand upside down*]

SUGGESTION: After children chant and perform this action song, you can call attention to words that mean the opposite (*pull* and *push*) and rhyming words (*town* and *down*).

I Love Chocolate

I love chocolate

Yum, yum, yum.

I love chocolate

In my tum.

SUGGESTION: Children will enjoy saying the poem over and over, substituting their favorite foods. Have them clap the syllables of each new food. Eventually you can use a printed version for shared reading.

I Measure Myself

I measure myself from my head to my toes,

I measure my arms, starting right by my nose,

I measure my legs, and I measure me all,

I measure to see if I'm growing tall.

SUGGESTION: After children learn the words, you can teach them movements to accompany each line: point from head to toe, point to nose and stretch out arms, point to length of legs, and stretch. Show children how to "measure" using a piece of yarn. They could work in partners to measure arms, legs, and so on. You can also read books about growing, such as *Titch* by Pat Hutchins.

I Scream

I scream,

You scream,

We all scream

For ice cream!

SUGGESTION: Compare the words *I scream* and *ice cream*, exaggerating and calling attention to the word breaks. Talk about how it helps to think about the meaning as you say the poem. Children can decorate a printed version of the poem with drawings of ice-cream cones.

I Stand on Tiptoe

I stand on tiptoe

To make myself tall.

I bend my knees

To make myself small.

But I like my sitting size best of all!

SUGGESTION: This verse is another good stretch activity to use between activities. For each line of the rhyme, have children add movement: stand on toes, stretch, bend knees, crouch, sit down. After the last line, the children will all be sitting on the rug in front of you.

fold
here

143

I Wiggle

I wiggle, wiggle, wiggle my fingers.

I wiggle, wiggle, wiggle my toes.

I wiggle, wiggle, wiggle my shoulders.

I wiggle, wiggle, wiggle my nose.

Now no more wiggles are left in me,

I am sitting as still as still can be.

ACTIONS:

I wiggle, wiggle, wiggle my fingers. [*wiggle fingers*]

I wiggle, wiggle, wiggle my toes. [*wiggle toes*]

I wiggle, wiggle, wiggle my shoulders. [*wiggle shoulders*]

I wiggle, wiggle, wiggle my nose. [*wiggle nose*]

Now no more wiggles are left in me, [*shake head*]

I am sitting as still as still can be. [*sit still*]

SUGGESTION: This simple, easy-to-remember poem, along with the accompanying actions, is easy for children to learn. Revisit it throughout the day. It's a fun transition activity as the children gather for a read-aloud or other whole-class activity.

If I Were a Bird

If I were a bird,

I'd sing a song,

And fly about

The whole day long,

And when the night came,

Go to rest,

Up in my cozy little nest.

SUGGESTION: Assign different groups to read particular lines. You can create a beautiful version of the poem on chart paper by having children decorate the border with drawings of birds. The top of the chart can show birds flying, and the bottom can show birds on nests.

fold
here

145

If You're Happy and You Know It

If you're happy and you know it, clap your hands.

If you're happy and you know it, clap your hands.

If you're happy and you know it, then your face

will surely show it.

If you're happy and you know it, clap your hands.

ADDITIONAL VERSES:

If you're happy and you know it, stomp your feet . . .

If you're happy and you know it, shout "Hurray!" . . .

If you're happy and you know it, do all three . . .

SUGGESTION: Children will enjoy performing the actions of this song. Repeating all three actions in sequence (or adding others) can be a memory game.

I'm a Choo-Choo Train

I'm a choo-choo train

Chugging down the track.

First I go forward,

Then I go back.

Now my bell is ringing,

Hear my whistle blow.

What a lot of noise I make

Everywhere I go!

ACTIONS:

I'm a choo-choo train [*bend arms at sides*]
Chugging down the track. [*rhythmically move arms*]
First I go forward, [*move forward*]
Then I go back. [*move backward*]

Now my bell is ringing, [*pretend to ring bell*]
Hear my whistle blow.
What a lot of noise I make [*cover ears*]
Everywhere I go!

SUGGESTION: A whistle makes a big hit when sounded in connection with this rhyme. You can blow the whistle and have children take turns ringing a bell as the class pantomimes the poem together. Margaret Wise Brown's picture book *Two Little Trains* and *Freight Train*, by Donald Crews, enrich the locomotive experience, particularly for children who are unfamiliar with trains.

I'm Dusty Bill

I'm Dusty Bill

From Vinegar Hill,

Never had a bath

And I never will.

SUGGESTION: Children will find this poem humorous. Say it quickly with expression, and say the last line louder than the other three.

I'm a Little Acorn Brown

I'm a little acorn brown,

Lying on the cold, cold ground.

Everyone walks over me,

That is why I'm cracked you see.

I'm a nut

In a rut.

I'm a nut

In a rut.

SUGGESTION: Have children recite the poem, clapping their hands or snapping their fingers—twice—after each of the last four lines. Show children an acorn and explain that it is a seed from which a tree grows.

fold
here

149

I'm a Little Teapot

I'm a little teapot, short and stout,

Here is my handle, here is my spout.

When I get all steamed up, I just shout:

Tip me over and pour me out.

SUGGESTION: This song is a natural to act out: put a hand on one hip to make a handle, hold out the other arm for a spout, then tip to one side as the tea pours out. Help children come up with their own variations, such as this one: *I'm a tube of toothpaste on the shelf, / I get so lonely all by myself. / When it's time for bed, then hear me shout: / Lift my cap off and squeeze me out!*

It's Raining

It's raining, it's pouring,

The old man is snoring;

He went to bed and bumped his head

And couldn't get up in the morning.

SUGGESTION: There are many rhymes about rain. Have the group sing this one as a round, the second group starting when the first group finishes line one. As an accompaniment, children may make rain sounds by tapping their fingers on desks or other objects, lightly at first, and then harder and harder to create a real storm!

The Itsy, Bitsy Spider

The itsy, bitsy spider

Climbed up the waterspout.

Down came the rain

And washed the spider out.

Out came the sun

And dried up all the rain.

And the itsy, bitsy spider

Climbed up the spout again.

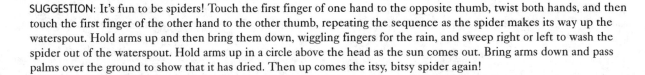

SUGGESTION: It's fun to be spiders! Touch the first finger of one hand to the opposite thumb, twist both hands, and then touch the first finger of the other hand to the other thumb, repeating the sequence as the spider makes its way up the waterspout. Hold arms up and then bring them down, wiggling fingers for the rain, and sweep right or left to wash the spider out of the waterspout. Hold arms up in a circle above the head as the sun comes out. Bring arms down and pass palms over the ground to show that it has dried. Then up comes the itsy, bitsy spider again!

Jack and Jill

Jack and Jill went up the hill

To get a pail of water;

Jack fell down and broke his crown,

And Jill came tumbling after.

SUGGESTION: Children may be unfamiliar with the idea of a *well*, so talk about it. Perhaps some of them have seen a well or drawn water from one. A word that may be confusing is *crown*. Thinking about where kings and queens wear their crowns helps children figure out what part of the body the "crown" is. After the children know the verse, have two children act out the parts as the rest of the class says it.

Jack, Be Nimble

Jack, be nimble,

Jack, be quick,

Jack, jump over

The candlestick.

SUGGESTION: Children enjoy discovering the meaning of *nimble*. Let children take turns jumping over a real or an imaginary candlestick. Or have them jump over a set of blocks or other low barrier instead. Substitute the name of the child who is jumping. Outside, have children chant the words as they jump over a rope held by two of their classmates. If everyone makes it over one height, raise the rope.

Jack-in-the-box

Jack-in-the-box,

Oh, so still.

Won't you come out?

Yes, I will.

ACTIONS:
Jack-in-the-box, [*tuck thumb in fist*]
Oh, so still. [*pause and stare at fist*]
Won't you come out? [*raise fist*]
Yes, I will. [*pop out thumb*]

SUGGESTION: Have children act this poem out as a finger play, bring in a real jack-in-the box, or have them make simple pop-up puppets: draw a jack-in-the-box character and cut it out; attach the puppet to a kraft stick or straw; thread the straw or stick through a Styrofoam cup with a hole in the bottom so that the puppet is hidden inside the cup; when it's time, push up the straw so that the puppet pops out.

fold
here

Jack, Jack

Jack, Jack, down you go,

Down in you box, down so low.

Jack, Jack, there goes the top,

Quickly now, up you pop!

SUGGESTION: Have one child squat behind a table or chair while you pantomime putting the top on. Then the child can jump up on the last line. Children's names can be substituted for *Jack*. As an alternative, use a real jack-in-the-box as you read the poem.

Jack Sprat

Jack Sprat could eat no fat.

His wife could eat no lean.

And so between them both, you see,

They licked the platter clean.

SUGGESTION: Assign a "soloist" for line 1, another "soloist" for line 2, and have the whole class read the final two lines. Introduce the idea of *opposites* and help children think of some other examples: day and night, fast and slow, big and little, and so forth.

fold here

157

Jerry Hall

Jerry Hall,

He is so small,

A rat could eat him,

Hat and all.

SUGGESTION: What would it be like to be very, very small? How would things look? Work together to make a new version about a different person with a different physical characteristic. A good book to use with this poem is *Mouse Views* by Bruce MacMillan.

Johnny Taps With One Hammer

Johnny taps with one hammer,

One hammer, one hammer,

Johnny taps with one hammer,

Then he taps with two.

SUGGESTION: After children are familiar with the verse, they can "count up" by adding verses. Repeat the verse substituting *two, three, four, five*. End by changing the last line to *Then he goes to bed*. Children can stand or sit in small groups of five. Let each child in the group recite one verse, substituting his or her own name. A more challenging task can be created by counting backward.

fold
here

Jumping Beans

One, two, three, four,

Beans came jumping through the door.

Five, six, seven, eight,

Jumping up onto my plate.

SUGGESTION: Children have a rollicking good time when they become jumping beans. Let them jump through the door, and position paper plates on the floor as bean "landing places." Ask children to hold up fingers or number cards as they chant the numbers.

Jumping Joan

Here I am, little jumping Joan.

When nobody's with me,

I'm always alone.

SUGGESTION: Have children draw themselves jumping, and arrange their drawings around the verse on a poetry chart. Discuss the idea that if no one is with you, then you would be by yourself, or *alone*.

fold here

161

Ladybug! Ladybug!

Ladybug! Ladybug!

Fly away home.

Your house is on fire

And your children are gone.

All except one,

And that's little Ann,

For she has crept under

The frying pan.

SUGGESTION: Have children substitute other rhyming words for *Ann* and *frying pan*—*Joan* and *telephone*, for example. Eric Carle's book *The Grouchy Ladybug* also features a ladybug.

Lazy Mary

Lazy Mary,

Will you get up,

Will you get up,

Will you get up?

Lazy Mary,

Will you get up

This cold and frosty morning?

No, no, mother

I won't get up,

I won't get up,

I won't get up,

No, no mother,

I won't get up

This cold and frosty morning.

SUGGESTION: Substitute other names as well as other words: *yes* and *I will* instead of *no* and *I won't*, other weather conditions for *cold* and *frosty*. How many weather words can children think of? Invite them to make a shared-writing list.

Little Ball

A little ball,

A bigger ball,

A great big ball I see.

Shall we count them?

Are you ready?

One,

Two,

Three.

SUGGESTION: Have children use actions to indicate the three sizes: make circle, with finger and thumb, with hands, and with arms. Or bring in three balls of different sizes and have a child bounce the appropriately sized one as the rest of the children chant the poem.

Little Bo-Peep

Little Bo-Peep has lost her sheep,

And doesn't know where to find them.

Leave them alone and they'll come home,

Wagging their tails behind them.

SUGGESTION: Divide the children into two groups and assign the first two lines to one group, and the last two lines to the other. Recite the first two lines sadly; then be joyful when the sheep return wagging their tails. Have a discussion about the simple story this poem tells.

fold
here

165

A Little Doggie

A little doggie,

All brown and black,

Wore his tail

Curled on his back.

SUGGESTION: This description of a little doggie is fun for children to draw and share. Have them invent other doggie details. Group the children's drawings around the printed poem on a poetry chart.

Little Fishes in a Brook

Little fishes in a brook,

Father caught them on a hook,

Mother fried them in a pan,

Johnnie ate them like a man.

SUGGESTION: Discuss the sequence of events in the simple story told in the poem. You can have four children volunteer to draw the events and arrange them next to the four lines of the poem.

fold here

167

Little Jack Horner

Little Jack Horner

Sat in a corner,

Eating his holiday pie;

He put in his thumb

And pulled out a plum,

And said, "What a good boy am I!"

SUGGESTION: Have children take turns being Jack (or Jackie). Children will have a lot to say about why Jack is eating pie with his thumb. And they may have lots of ideas about a holiday pie. What could it be? Have children draw, dictate, and write their ideas. These "recipes" are fun to share.

Little Jack Sprat

Little Jack Sprat

Once had a pig.

It was not very little,

It was not very big.

It was not very lean,

It was not very fat,

"It's a good pig to grunt,"

Said little Jack Sprat.

SUGGESTION: Children will enjoy this variation, particularly if they already know the traditional verse (see "Jack Sprat," in this volume). Point out that *grunt* is a word for the sound pigs make. Discuss words in the poem that are opposites.

fold
here

Little Miss Muffet

Little Miss Muffet

Sat on a tuffet,

Eating her curds and whey;

Along came a spider,

And sat down beside her,

And frightened Miss Muffet away!

SUGGESTION: This poem tells a story that can be acted out. Children may like to talk about whether they like spiders or are scared of them. They may be interested to learn that *curds and whey* is similar to cottage cheese.

Little Miss Tucket

Little Miss Tucket

Sat on a bucket,

Eating her peaches and cream;

There came a grasshopper

Who tried hard to stop her

But she said, "Go away or I'll scream!"

SUGGESTION: Once children know "Little Miss Muffet," they will find this variation amusing.

Little Mouse

Walk little mouse, walk little mouse.

Hide little mouse, hide little mouse.

Here comes the cat!

Run little mouse, run little mouse!

SUGGESTION: Have the children accompany the verse with actions: tiptoe around, cover eyes with hands, look around, run away. Or act out the story: lots of mice and one cat equals a great creative dramatic activity. Doing this outside generates some great chases! Children can also substitute other action words (*crawl, skip, kneel, jump*).

Little Paul Parrot

Little Paul Parrot

Sat in his garret,

Eating toast and tea;

A little brown mouse

Jumped into the house,

And stole the toast for me.

SUGGESTION: Invite two children, one playing the parrot and the other the mouse, to act out the rhyme as the group says it. Children can tell the story of the poem. You may want to discuss how *garret* is similar to an attic or top floor.

Little Red Apple

A little red apple grew high in a tree.

I looked up at it.

It looked down at me.

"Come down, please," I said.

And that little red apple fell right on my head.

ACTIONS:
A little red apple grew high in a tree. [*point up*]
I looked up at it. [*shade eyes and look up*]
It looked down at me. [*shade eyes and look down*]
"Come down, please," I said. [*motion downward*]
And that little red apple fell right on my head. [*tap top of head*]

SUGGESTION: Teach children this verse and the finger and hand movements that go along with it. They can also talk about the story the poem tells and discuss whether an apple could really "look down." They may conclude that the speaker was wishing for an apple and one happened to fall.

Little Robin Redbreast

Little robin redbreast,

Stay upon a rail.

Niddle-noodle went his head,

Wibble-wobble went his tail.

ACTIONS:
Little robin redbreast,
Stay upon a rail. [*hold up thumb and little finger and curl down rest of fingers*]
Niddle-noodle went his head, [*wiggle thumb*]
Wibble-wobble went his tail. [*wiggle little finger*]

SUGGESTION: Have children recite the poem as they perform the finger actions described above. Children love nonsense words like *niddle-noodle* and *wibble-wobble*. Ask them to invent other nonsense words that fit the actions of the verse. English-language learners may need to see a photograph of a robin and other birds.

Little Snail

The snail is so slow,

The snail is so slow.

He creeps along

And creeps along.

The snail is

So-o s-l-o-w.

SUGGESTION: Sing this verse to the tune of "The Farmer in the Dell," or simply recite it, saying the last two words very, very slowly.

Little Tommy Tucker

Little Tommy Tucker sings for his supper.

What shall he sing for?

White bread and butter.

How shall he cut it without any knife?

How shall he marry without any wife?

SUGGESTION: There are all kinds of puzzles in this verse. What could it mean for a child to "sing for his supper"? And how could he cut bread without a knife? Children enjoy trying to unravel these mysteries as they enjoy the rhythm and rhyme.

fold here

177

Little White Rabbit

Little white rabbit,

Hop on one foot, one foot.

Little white rabbit,

Hop on two feet, two feet.

Little white rabbit,

Hop on three feet, three feet.

Little white rabbit,

Hop on four feet, four feet.

Little white rabbit,

Hop, hop, hop.

SUGGESTION: This poem is a good counting rhyme. Children can substitute other colors in place of *white* (*brown, black, gray*).

London Bridge

London Bridge is falling down,

Falling down, falling down,

London Bridge is falling down,

My fair lady.

ADDITIONAL VERSES:

Build it up with wood and clay,
Wood and clay, wood and clay,
Build it up with wood and clay,
My fair lady.

Wood and clay will wash away,
Wash away, wash away,
Wood and clay will wash away,
My fair lady.

Build it up with iron bars,
Iron bars, iron bars.
Build it up with iron bars,
My fair lady.

Iron bars will bend and break,
Bend and break, bend and break.
Iron bars will bend and break,
My fair lady.

SUGGESTION: Play a game in which two children form a bridge by joining their hands, both arms stretched upward. Ask the other children to march under the arch in single file as they sing the song. On "My fair lady" the arch falls, capturing a child, who becomes an observer. Continue until all children have been caught.

The Lost Shoe

Doodle, doodle, do,

The princess lost her shoe.

Her highness hopped,

The fiddler stopped,

Not knowing what to do.

SUGGESTION: Have children demonstrate how you might hop on one foot if you lost a shoe. Explain to children that *her highness* is what you might call a princess.

Lucy Locket

Lucy Locket lost her pocket,

Kitty Fisher found it;

Not a penny was there in it,

Only ribbon 'round it.

SUGGESTION: Emphasize the meter by tapping a rhythm stick while the children say/read the poem (let children join in on rereadings). Have two teams or groups split the poem by taking turns—one says the first and third lines, the other responds with the second and fourth lines. Explain that a *pocket* in this poem is a purse or a pocketbook.

fold
here

181

Make a Pancake

Make a pancake, pat, pat, pat.

Do not make it fat, fat, fat.

You must make it flat, flat, flat.

Make a pancake just like that.

SUGGESTION: Have children perform actions as they say the rhyme: pat hands together, stretch hands apart, pat hands together, clap hands together. Print the words to this rhyme on a poetry chart and read and illustrate the poem together. Have children put pocket chart strips in order to re-create the poem. Once children know the poem, give them a printed version so they can notice and highlight the *-at* phonogram.

The Man in the Moon

The Man in the Moon looked out of the moon,

Looked out of the moon and said,

"It's time for all children on the Earth

To think about getting to bed!"

SUGGESTION: Children love to chant and illustrate this rhyme. Here's a slightly different version, in which you can discuss what is meant by the moon "getting up": *The Man in the Moon | looked out of the moon, | And this is what he said, | "tis time that, | now I'm getting up, | All babies went to bed!"*

fold here

183

Mary Ann, Mary Ann

Mary Ann, Mary Ann

Make the porridge in a pan.

Make it thick, make it thin,

Make it any way you can.

SUGGESTION: Substitute different names that include *Ann* such as *Betty Ann, Peggy Ann,* or *Carol Ann;* invite the children to guess what *porridge* is (something like oatmeal). If children are working with a printed version of the poem, you can draw their attention to the *-an* phonogram.

Mary Had a Little Lamb

Mary had a little lamb,

Its fleece was white as snow,

And everywhere that Mary went

The lamb was sure to go.

It followed her to school one day,

Which was against the rule.

It made the children laugh and play

To see a lamb at school.

SUGGESTION: Have children draw, dictate, or write a story about Mary and her lamb. A terrific follow-up to this poem is Tomie de Paola's picture book *Mary Had a Little Lamb*, or Bruce MacMillan's *Mary Had a Little Lamb*, both of which tell the whole story and offer excellent visuals for English-language learners. The verse can also be sung to the tune of "Merrily We Roll Along."

Mary, Mary, Quite Contrary

Mary, Mary, quite contrary,

How does your garden grow?

With silver bells and cockleshells,

And pretty maids all in a row.

SUGGESTION: What does it mean to be *contrary*? Have children discuss this concept and tell about when they have acted this way. Tell children that *silver bells* are a kind of flower and *cockleshells* are marine mollusks, and ask them what they think they are doing in the garden. Substitute class members' names for *Mary*.

Mary Wore Her Red Dress

Mary wore her red dress, red dress, red dress.

Mary wore her red dress

All day long.

Mary wore her red hat, red hat, red hat.

Mary wore her red hat

All day long.

Mary wore her red shoes, red shoes, red shoes.

Mary wore her red shoes

All day long.

ADDITIONAL VERSES:

Mary wore her red gloves, red gloves, red gloves . . .

Mary was a red bird, red bird, red bird . . .

SUGGESTION: This poem can be adapted in numerous ways as suggested by Merle Peeke in *Mary Wore Her Red Dress and Henry Wore His Green Sneakers*. Children can substitute their names, various colors, and their favorite clothing.

fold here

Milkman, Milkman

Milkman, Milkman, where have you been?

In Buttermilk Channel up to my chin.

I spilt my milk and I spoiled my clothes,

And I got a long icicle hung from my nose.

SUGGESTION: Explain that a *channel* is a body of water like a river. Have children think about a man in a channel in cold weather. Children may enjoy saying *milk*, *milkman*, and *buttermilk* as well as related words.

Mix a Pancake

by Christina Rossetti

Mix a pancake,

Stir a pancake,

Pop it in the pan;

Fry the pancake,

Toss the pancake—

Catch it if you can.

SUGGESTION: This is a great poem for children to pantomime mixing, stirring, popping, frying, tossing, and catching pancakes. This poem pairs well with Tomie de Paola's wordless picture book *Pancakes for Breakfast*. Children enjoy predicting what happens next.

The Mocking Bird

Hush, little baby, don't say a word,

Papa's going to buy you a mocking bird.

If the mocking bird won't sing,

Papa's going to buy you a diamond ring.

If the diamond ring turns to brass,

Papa's going to buy you a looking glass.

If the looking glass gets broke,

Papa's going to buy you a billy goat.

If that billy goat runs away,

Papa's going to buy you a bale of hay.

SUGGESTION: Sing this song with the children. Some children may need help with the vocabulary *mocking bird, looking glass, billy goat,* and *bale of hay.* Ask children to help you create additional verses to this lullaby.

Muffin Man

Oh, do you know the muffin man,

The muffin man, the muffin man?

Oh, do you know the muffin man

Who lives on Drury Lane?

Oh, yes I know the muffin man,

The muffin man, the muffin man.

Oh, yes, I know the muffin man

Who lives on Drury Lane.

SUGGESTION: Have one group of children sing the first verse and another group sing the second verse. When all the children are familiar with the words, turn this into a game full of suspense: blindfold one class member, have the class sing the first verse, point to one child to sing the second verse as a solo, give the blindfolded child three guesses to name the soloist; then blindfold the soloist and continue the game.

My Apple

Look at my apple, it is nice and round.

It fell from a tree, down to the ground.

Come, let me share my apple, please do!

My mother can cut it half in two—

One half for me and one half for you.

SUGGESTION: Have children learn this verse and accompanying line-by-line hand motions: cup hands, move fingers in a downward motion, make a beckoning motion, make a slicing motion, hold out two hands offering the two halves.

My Dog, Rags

I have a dog and his name is Rags,

He eats so much that his tummy sags,

His ears flip-flop and his tail wig-wags,

And when he walks he zig-zig-zags!

ACTIONS:

I have a dog and his name is Rags, [*point to self*]

He eats so much that his tummy sags, [*put hands together in front of stomach*]

His ears flip-flop and his tail wig-wags, [*bend each hand at wrist*]

And when he walks he zig-zig-zags! [*make an imaginary Z with index finger*]

SUGGESTION: Have children learn the words of this verse and the motions to accompany it. If you are using a printed version, call attention to the phonogram -*ag* with the plural -*s*.

My Eyes Can See

My eyes can see.

My mouth can talk.

My ears can hear.

My feet can walk.

My nose can sniff.

My teeth can chew.

My eyelids can blink.

My arms can hug you.

SUGGESTION: Children will naturally want to act out the words being said. You can use a drawing of a person with this poem, pointing to the parts of the body.

My Head

This is the circle that is my head.

This is my mouth with which words are said.

These are my eyes with which I see.

This is my nose that is part of me.

This is the hair that grows on my head,

And this is my hat I wear on my head.

SUGGESTION: Have children point to or otherwise indicate on their own faces each feature as it is mentioned. You can also use an enlarged drawing or a photo of a face.

My Little Sister

My little sister dressed in pink

Washed all the dishes in the sink.

How many dishes did she break?

One, two, three, four, five.

SUGGESTION: Help children develop their vocabulary by coming up with variations: *My little brother dressed in blue | Washed all the animals at the zoo*, and so on. Ask class members to suggest actions to perform when saying each number: jumping, hopping, spinning, popping up.

Old MacDonald Had a Farm

Old MacDonald had a farm,

E - I - E - I - O

And on this farm he had a cow,

E - I - E - I - O

With a moo, moo here,

And a moo, moo there,

Here a moo, there a moo,

Everywhere a moo, moo,

Old MacDonald had a farm,

E - I - E - I - O.

SUGGESTION: Teach the song, and then have children add more verses featuring other animals and the noises they make: pig—oink, oink; cat—meow, meow; dog—bow-wow; horse—neigh, neigh. Accompany the verses with motions representative of the different animals. Make each verse cumulative, repeating all the animal noises each time. Sing a version of the song in which the farm owner is female: "Mom MacDonald had a farm. . . ." Follow up by reading *Ms. MacDonald Has a Class*, by Jan Ormerod.

Oliver Twist

Oliver Twist, can you do this?

If so, do so.

Number one, touch your tongue.

Number two, touch your shoe.

Number three, touch your knee.

Number four, touch the floor.

Number five, jump up high.

SUGGESTION: Once children are familiar with the rhyme, have them work with a partner. One partner recites the poem, and the other twists continuously while performing the actions. Then the partners switch roles. Have children come up with their own actions for Oliver Twist to do. After children have played around with "Oliver Twist," introduce this nonsense variation: *Oliver Twist couldn't do this. / What's the use of trying so? / Give him my toe. Over you go. / Oliver, Oliver Twisteo.*

One for Sorrow

One for sorrow

Two for joy

Three for a girl

Four for a boy

Five for silver

Six for gold

Seven for a secret

Never to be told.

SUGGESTION: After children have heard this poem a few times, assign each line to individual children. Have them practice saying their parts and then practice, as a group, their ability to present the poem smoothly and in order. Revisit this poem when children are locating numerals and number words in text.

fold
here

One Potato, Two Potato

One potato, two potato,

Three potato, four,

Five potato, six potato,

Seven potato more,

Eight potato, nine potato,

Where is ten?

Now we must count over again.

SUGGESTION: Have children make two fists and alternate tapping one on top of the other as they recite this rhyme. The rhyme can also be used in a counting game. Have children stand in a circle, one player in the middle. The children in the circle hold out two fists each. The player in the middle taps alternate fists, in sequence, each time she or he says a number word or the word *more*. Tapped fists go behind backs. The winner is the last player to have both fists eliminated.

One, Two, Buckle My Shoe

One, two,

Buckle my shoe.

Three, four,

Knock at the door.

Five, six,

Pick up sticks.

Seven, eight,

Lay them straight.

Nine, ten,

A big fat hen.

SUGGESTION: This is an easy counting rhyme, with specific motions that can be pantomimed for each pair of numbers. After children know the rhyme, write it on a chart using numerals in place of the number words. You may want to make a big book with five pages—one for every pair of lines—or five-page little books for children to illustrate.

fold
here

201

One, Two, Three, Four

One, two, three, four

Mary's at the cottage door,

Five, six, seven, eight,

Eating cherries off a plate.

SUGGESTION: Have one group chant the first and third lines, a second group respond with the alternate lines. Substitute other names for *Mary*. Invite a child to act out *Eating cherries off a plate*.

Open, Shut Them

Open, shut them,

Open, shut them,

Give a little clap.

Open, shut them.

Open, shut them.

ADDITIONAL VERSES:

ADDITIONAL VERSES:

Creep them, creep them,	Roll them, roll them,	Faster, faster,
Creep them, creep them,	Roll them, roll them,	Faster, faster,
Right up to your chin.	To your shoulders fly.	Give a little clap.
Open up your mouth.	Then like little birdies,	Slower, slower, slower, slower,
But do not let them in.	Let them flutter to the sky.	Lay them in your lap.
Crawl them, crawl them,	Falling, falling,	
Crawl them, crawl them,	Falling, falling,	
Give a little shriek.	Right down to the ground.	
Open wide your shining eyes.	Quickly pick them up again,	
And through your fingers peek.	And turn them 'round and 'round.	

SUGGESTION: Children will enjoy the hand movements of the actions in this poem: opening and shutting both hands, putting them in their laps, creeping them up to their chins and then eyes, and then rolling them and fluttering them high.

Papa's Glasses

These are Papa's glasses.

This is Papa's hat.

This is how he folds his hands

And puts them in his lap.

ACTIONS:
These are Papa's glasses. [*make glasses with fingers*]
This is Papa's hat. [*tent hands on head*]
This is how he folds his hands [*fold hands*]
And puts them in his lap. [*place hands in lap*]

fold
here

SUGGESTION: Have the children complete the actions along with the rhyme. Create new verses about Nana's or Grandma's glasses.

Pat-a-cake

Pat-a-cake, pat-a-cake, baker's man,

Bake me a cake as fast as you can.

Pat it and prick it and mark it with B,

And put it in the oven for Tommy and me.

SUGGESTION: Have children recite this rhyme in pairs. For the first two lines, pat hands on thighs, clap hands together at chest level, then put hands out, palms up, to pat partner's hands. For line 3, mime patting, pricking, and writing a B in the air. For line 4, mime putting the cake in the oven, and then pretend to cradle a baby back and forth.

fold here

205

A Peanut Sat on a Railroad Track

A peanut sat on a railroad track,

Its heart was all a-flutter.

Around the bend

Came Number Ten

Toot! Toot! Peanut butter!

SUGGESTION: *Toot! Toot!* is just one sound the train can make as it comes down the railroad track. Children can incorporate other sound effects, such as a bell, tambourine, whistle, and even other words, such as *chooo-chooo, ch-ch-ch-ch*, and *whooo-oo-oo-ooo*. Motions can show a heart "a-flutter" and the approaching train. For a grand finale, children can smash their hands together on *Peanut butter!*

Peas

I eat my peas with honey,

I've done it all my life.

It makes the peas taste funny,

But it keeps them on the knife.

SUGGESTION: This poem conjures up a comical image: peas balanced on a knife. Have children draw a picture of this or act it out. Replace *peas* with other foods that are hard to balance on a knife, such as grapes. As they become familiar with the structure of the rhyme, ask them to try to create verses about other food items and/or eating utensils. (See *Beets* in this volume.)

Pease Porridge Hot

Pease porridge hot,

Pease porridge cold,

Pease porridge in the pot,

Nine days old.

Some like it hot,

Some like it cold,

Some like it in the pot,

Nine days old.

ACTIONS:

Pease porridge hot, [*clap own hands*]
Pease porridge cold, [*clap partner's hands*]
Pease porridge in the pot, [*clap own hands*]
Nine days old. [*clap partner's hands*]

Some like it hot, [*one fist on top of the other*]
Some like it cold, [*alternate fists, placing the other on top*]
Some like it in the pot, [*clap partner's hands*]
Nine days old. [*clap own hands*]

SUGGESTION: This is a real snappy, clappy poem! Have children perform the actions, or have children divide into two groups to recite and perform alternate lines or alternate stanzas.

Peter, Peter, Pumpkin-eater

Peter, Peter, pumpkin-eater,

Had a wife and couldn't keep her.

He put her in a pumpkin shell,

And there he kept her very well.

SUGGESTION: What is a pumpkin-eater? What does a pumpkin-eater have to do with the poem? What would it be like to live in a pumpkin house? A pumpkin-shell home is an image that is fun to draw.

fold
here

209

Point to the Right

Point to the right of me.

Point to the left of me.

Point up above me.

Point down below.

Right, left, up,

And down so slow.

SUGGESTION: Have children use both arms to point in the directions indicated. Emphasize saying the poem with expression, slowing down on the last line.

Polly Put the Kettle On

Polly put the kettle on,

Polly put the kettle on,

Polly put the kettle on,

We'll all have tea.

Sukey take it off again,

Sukey take it off again,

Sukey take it off again,

They've all gone away.

SUGGESTION: Discuss the story this poem tells. If children are working with a printed version, draw attention to the repeated phrases. Children can even underline or highlight these phrases.

Pop! Goes the Weasel

All around the cobbler's bench,

The monkey chased the weasel;

The monkey thought it was all in fun,

Pop! goes the weasel.

A penny for a spool of thread,

A penny for a needle;

That's the way the money goes,

Pop! goes the weasel.

SUGGESTION: The surprise ending of each verse is irresistible: children can't wait to pop up! Some children may not be familiar with the words *weasel* and *cobbler*.

Puppies and Kittens

One little, two little, three little kittens

Were napping in the sun.

One little, two little, three little puppies

Said, "Let's have some fun."

Up to the kittens the puppies went creeping,

As quiet as could be.

One little, two little, three little kittens

Went scampering up a tree!

ACTIONS:
One little, two little, three little kittens [*pop up three fingers*]
Were napping in the sun. [*rest head on hands*]
One little, two little, three little puppies [*pop up three fingers*]
Said, "Let's have some fun." [*smile*]

Up to the kittens the puppies went creeping, [*creep right fingers up left arm*]
As quiet as could be. [*hold an index finger up to lips*]
One little, two little, three little kittens [*pop up three fingers*]
Went scampering up a tree! [*wiggle fingers overhead*]

SUGGESTION: The great vocabulary in this poem—*napping, creeping, scampering*—can be reinforced by miming the actions.

Pussycat, Pussycat

"Pussycat, pussycat, where have you been?"

"I've been to London to visit the Queen!"

"Pussycat, pussycat, what did you do there?"

"I frightened a little mouse under her chair."

SUGGESTION: Learn the verse as a whole group, and then have one group of children read the questions and the others respond. Or children can recite it with a partner. If you are using a printed version, you may want to point out the use of quotation marks in this poem. Ask whether children have noticed quotations marks in books you've read together, and discuss what they mean.

Rain on the Rooftops

Rain on the rooftops,

Rain on the trees,

Rain on the green grass,

But not on me!

SUGGESTION: After children learn this verse, they will enjoy thinking of imaginative places it could rain, making their own rhymes. Substitute other words for *rain*, such as *snow*, *hail*, *sleet*, or *sunshine*.

fold
here

215

Rain, Rain, Go Away

Rain, rain, go away,

Come again another day.

Rain, rain, go away.

Little _____ wants to play.

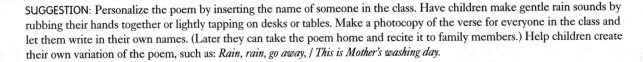

SUGGESTION: Personalize the poem by inserting the name of someone in the class. Have children make gentle rain sounds by rubbing their hands together or lightly tapping on desks or tables. Make a photocopy of the verse for everyone in the class and let them write in their own names. (Later they can take the poem home and recite it to family members.) Help children create their own variation of the poem, such as: *Rain, rain, go away, | This is Mother's washing day.*

Red, White, and Blue

Red, white, and blue,

Tap me on the shoe.

Red, white, and green,

Tap me on the bean.

Red, white, and black,

Tap me on the back.

SUGGESTION: One way to help children memorize poems and songs is by using the "echo" technique: say a line, have children repeat it, and after every two or three lines have them say everything they've learned so far. Have the children perform the motions as they say the words of this poem. Invite them to create new verses using different colors and rhyming words: *red/head*, *brown/frown*, for example.

fold here

217

Ride a Cock-horse

Ride a cock-horse

To Banbury Cross,

To see a fine lady

Upon a white horse;

Rings on her fingers

And bells on her toes,

She shall have music

Wherever she goes.

SUGGESTION: The words and rhythm of this poem mimic the sound of hoofbeats. Let children mark the beat by clapping their hands or tapping their fingers on their palms. Have different groups read each line. Children can imagine how the fine lady would look with rings on her fingers and bells on her toes.

Rig-a-jig-jig

Thumbkin, pointer, middleman big,

Silly man, wee man,

Rig-a-jig-jig.

SUGGESTION: Have children touch the appropriate digit of each hand together as they name it and then roll their hands around as they say *rig-a-jig-jig*.

fold
here

219

Ring Around the Rosie

Ring around the rosie,

A pocket full of posies,

Ashes! Ashes!

We all fall down.

SUGGESTION: Have children join hands in a circle and walk in one direction as they say the words. The exciting highlight of this game comes with the words *all fall down:* everyone sits down on the floor! Then they can chant the verse again walking in the reverse direction.

The Rooster

Cock-a-doodle-do!

The rooster flaps his wings,

Cock-a-doodle-do!

He flaps his wings and sings,

Cock-a-doodle-do!

The rooster sings and then,

Cock-a-doodle-do!

Cock-a-doodle-do!

He flaps his wings again.

SUGGESTION: Use sounds from simple instruments such as a xylophone or tambourine to accompany the *cock-a-doodle-do*s!

Roses Are Red

Roses are red,

Violets are blue,

Sugar is sweet,

And so are you.

SUGGESTION: See how many other kinds of flowers the class can name. Anita Lobel's picture book *Allison's Zinnia* introduces many flowers, as does Lois Ehlert's *Planting a Rainbow*. Make new versions of the poem using other categories, colors, and descriptions: *Tomatoes are red, | Blueberries are blue, | Corn is yellow, | Violets for you.*

Row, Row, Row Your Boat

Row, row, row your boat

Gently down the stream;

Merrily, merrily, merrily, merrily,

Life is but a dream.

Row, row, row your boat

Down the jungle stream;

If you see a crocodile,

Don't forget to scream!

SUGGESTION: Have children sing this song as they mime rowing. When they know the song well, they can sing it as a round. The first group starts singing (and keeps going), the second group begins when the first finishes the second line. Here's a variation: *Rock, rock, rock your boat | Gently to and fro; | Watch out! Give a shout, | In the water you go!*

fold here

Sally, Go 'Round

Sally, go 'round the sun,

Sally, go 'round the moon,

Sally, go 'round the chimney pots

Every afternoon.

BUMP!

SUGGESTION: See John Langstaff's book *Sally Go 'Round the Sun* for the music to this and similar songs. Children love to spin as they say this rhyme and at the end suddenly spin in the other direction. Or have them make a circle and skip to the left, reversing when they say "BUMP!"

See-Saw, Marjorie Daw

See-saw, Marjorie Daw,

Jack will have a new master;

He shall have but a penny a day,

Because he won't work any faster.

SUGGESTION: Who knows what this poem means (one version reads: *See-saw, Marjorie Daw,* | *Sold her bed and lay upon straw*), but there's magic in saying it together and enjoying the way the words rhyme. Have children make up their own stories about Marjorie Daw and Jack.

Sing, Sing

Sing, sing,

What will I sing?

The cat ran away

With the pudding string!

Do, do,

What will I do?

The cat ran away

With the pudding, too!

SUGGESTION: Children may have difficulty understanding how *pudding* (which to them is a dessert) could have a string. Explain that in olden times *pudding* was a sausage (like a hot dog) with a string at the end. It's interesting that the cat ran away with both.

Six Little Ducks

Six little ducks that I once knew,

Fat ducks, pretty ducks they were too,

But the one little duck with the feather on his back,

He led the others with his quack-quack-quack.

Down to the meadow they would go,

Wig-wag, wiggle-wag, to and fro,

But the one little duck with the feather on his back,

He led the others with his quack-quack-quack.

SUGGESTION: Children love both animal noises and nonsense words. This rhyme has both. Children love to *wig-wag, wiggle-wag* and, of course, *quack-quack-quack*. Substitute other adjectives for *fat* and *pretty* in line 2.

Skip to My Lou

Lou, Lou, skip to my Lou,

Lou, Lou, skip to my Lou,

Lou, Lou, skip to my Lou,

Skip to my Lou, my darling!

Refrain

Skip, skip, skip to my Lou,

Skip, skip, skip to my Lou,

Skip, skip, skip to my Lou,

Skip to my Lou, my darling!

ADDITIONAL VERSES:

Lost my partner, what'll I do?
Lost my partner, what'll I do?
Lost my partner, what'll I do?
Skip to my Lou, my darling!

Refrain

I'll find another one, that I'll do,
I'll find another one, that I'll do,
I'll find another one, that I'll do,
Skip to my Lou, my darling!

Refrain

Can't get a red bird, blue bird'll do,
Can't get a red bird, blue bird'll do,
Can't get a red bird, blue bird'll do,
Skip to my Lou, my darling!

Refrain

Flies in the sugar bowl, shoo, shoo, shoo,
Flies in the sugar bowl, shoo, shoo, shoo,
Flies in the sugar bowl, shoo, shoo, shoo,
Skip to my Lou, my darling!

Refrain

SUGGESTION: This is an old circle-game song (and a great "piggyback tune" to make up new words for). Children, in pairs, stand in a circle, with one child in the center. They all clap as they sing the chorus. On the words, "Lost my partner," the child in the center chooses a partner from the circle. These two children skip around the outside of the circle while the rest of the children clap and sing. The child whose partner was taken moves to the center and sings, "I'll find another one," chooses a partner, and together they skip around the outside. This sequence continues with the remaining verses.

Slippery Soap

Slippery, slippery, slippery soap!

Now you see it, now you don't.

Slide it on your arms, one, two, three,

Now your arms are slippery!

Slide it on your legs, one, two, three,

Now your legs are slippery!

SUGGESTION: The beginning letters in the words *slippery soap* sound "slippery" and "slick." On some lines say *slippery* quickly and on others say *slip-per-y* slowly. Have children let imaginary soap bars slip out of their hands as they recite the first line of the poem. Sliding, slithering actions will come naturally as they manipulate the invisible soap bars around their arms and legs. Have them repeat the rhyme, inserting different parts of the body: *toes, knees, knuckles, elbows, ankles*. If they insert a singular body part, like *neck*, remind them to change the verb to singular: *is*.

Snail, Snail

Snail, snail,

Put out your horns,

And I'll give you bread

And barleycorns.

SUGGESTION: Have children create a snail by making a fist, thumb tucked inside, and then lifting the little finger and index finger to make the horns.

Someone's Birthday

Today is a birthday,

I wonder for whom.

We know it's somebody

Who's right in this room.

So look all around you

For somebody who

Is laughing and smiling

My goodness—it's you!

SUGGESTION: After reading the poem, place a special hat or button on the child whose birthday it is. Invite the birthday child to choose a story for the group read-aloud.

fold here

231

Sometimes

Sometimes I am tall,

Sometimes I am small.

Sometimes I am very, very, tall,

Sometimes I am very, very, small.

Sometimes tall,

Sometimes small.

Sometimes neither tall nor small.

SUGGESTION: Have children act out the ideas of *small* and *tall* in the rhyme: stand tall, crouch low, stand on tiptoes, crouch and lower head, stand tall, crouch down, stand straight. Teach measurement in connection with this chant: measure the children at the beginning of the school year and record their heights on a chart; then measure and record their heights again midyear and at the end of the year so that children see real evidence of *small* and *tall*.

Stop, Look, and Listen

Stop, look, and listen

Before you cross the street.

First use your eyes and ears,

Then use your feet.

SUGGESTION: After children learn this poem, have them add hand and foot movements: for the first line, they *stop* by
thrusting their hand out in front of them as if they were stopping traffic, turn their heads left and right to *look* both ways,
and then cup one ear with their hands to *listen*. For the second line, they hold one arm out, palm down and elbow bent, and
use two fingers of the other hand to indicate a walking motion across the outstretched arm. For the third line, they hold up
one finger to indicate *first* and use that same finger to point to their eyes and ears. They walk in place for the final line.

Stretch

Stretch to the windows,

Stretch to the door,

Stretch up to the ceiling,

And bend to the floor.

SUGGESTION: Have children perform the stated actions as they chant the words, pointing to areas in the classroom (*window, door, ceiling, floor*).

Stretching Fun

I stretch and stretch and find it fun

To try to reach up to the sun.

I bend and bend to touch the ground,

Then I twist and twist around.

SUGGESTION: Children get some good stretching exercise as they say the rhyme and perform the stated actions. Have children say *stretch* and *touch* or *ground* and *around* to notice they have the same ending sounds.

fold
here

235

Teddy Bear, Teddy Bear

Teddy bear, teddy bear,
Turn around.

Teddy bear, teddy bear,
Touch the ground.

Teddy bear, teddy bear,
Touch your shoe.

Teddy bear, teddy bear,
Say howdy-do.

Teddy bear, teddy bear,
Turn out the light.

Teddy bear, teddy bear,
Say good night.

SUGGESTION: Have children perform the actions in this poem. Repetition of the first line makes it easy to learn the verses, or have children make up their own verses and actions.

Teeter-totter

Teeter-totter, bread and water,

I'll be the son and you be the daughter.

Teeter-totter, bread and water,

I'll eat the bread and you drink the water.

SUGGESTION: Have children in partners imitate the up-and-down motion of the teeter-totter as they say the poem.

fold
here

237

Ten Little Fingers

I have ten little fingers,

And they all belong to me.

I can make them do things.

Do you want to see?

I can make them point,

I can make them hold,

I can make them dance,

And then I make them fold.

ACTIONS:

I have ten little fingers, [*hold up ten fingers*]
And they all belong to me. [*point to self*]
I can make them do things. [*wiggle fingers*]
Do you want to see? [*tilt head*]

I can make them point, [*point*]
I can make them hold, [*hold fingertips together*]
I can make them dance, [*dance fingers on arm*]
And then I make them fold. [*fold hands in lap*]

fold
here

SUGGESTION: Have the children perform the actions indicated above. They can end by counting all ten fingers and then folding them again.

There Once Was a Queen

There once was a queen

Whose face was green.

She ate her milk

And drank her bread,

And got up in the morning

To go to bed.

SUGGESTION: Invite the children to discuss what makes this poem funny. What words would they change to make it not funny?

fold
here

239

There Was an Old Lady Who Swallowed a Fly

There was an old lady who swallowed a fly.

I don't know why she swallowed the fly.

Perhaps she'll die.

There was an old lady who swallowed a spider

That wriggled and jiggled and tickled inside her.

She swallowed the spider to catch the fly.

I don't know why she swallowed the fly.

Perhaps she'll die.

ADDITIONAL VERSES:

There was an old lady who swallowed a bird.
How absurd! She swallowed a bird.

She swallowed the bird to catch…
etc.

There was an old lady who swallowed a cat.
Think of that! She swallowed a cat.

She swallowed the cat to catch…
etc.

There was an old lady who swallowed a dog.
What a hog! She swallowed a dog.

She swallowed the dog to catch…
etc.

There was an old lady who swallowed a goat.
It stuck in her throat! She swallowed a goat.

She swallowed the goat to catch…
etc.

There was an old lady who swallowed a horse.
She died, of course.

SUGGESTION: Teach the children the song and make it cumulative by adding each new verse. You can make an old lady from an open paper bag by adding arms, legs, and a head. Let children draw and cut out all the things the old lady ate. They love to feed her, stuffing the bag and chanting the rhyme.

There Was an Old Woman

There was an old woman,

Who lived under a hill.

And if she's not gone,

She lives there still.

SUGGESTION: Help children understand the last two lines of the poem. (A different way to say those two lines is that the old woman is still living there.) Say the lines of the poem quickly, clapping at the rhyming words *hill* and *still*.

fold
here

241

There Was an Old Woman Who Lived in a Shoe

There was an old woman

Who lived in a shoe,

She had so many children

She didn't know what to do.

She gave them some soup

With butter and bread,

Kissed them all fondly

And put them to bed.

SUGGESTION: Create a written version of this familiar verse and illustrate it with a large shoe. You can put small photos of the children in the shoe or have them draw and cut out pictures of themselves. They will enjoy taking turns reading the poem with a pointer after they know it.

This Is the Way We Go to School

This is the way we go to school,

Go to school, go to school.

This is the way we go to school,

On a cold and frosty morning.

SUGGESTION: Children can sing this song and act it out very creatively, especially as a transition between activities. Make up your own verses: *this is the way we start the day, go to lunch, take a nap, read a book, tie our shoes,* and so forth. They can also change the song to suit the weather (*warm and sunny morning*).

fold here

243

This Is the Way We Wash Our Face

This is the way we wash our face,

Wash our face, wash our face,

This is the way we wash our face,

Until we're squeaky clean.

SUGGESTION: Have children sing this to the tune of "Here We Go 'Round the Mulberry Bush." Children will probably spontaneously mime washing their faces. Once they are familiar with the repetitive pattern, create new verses by substituting new body parts: *cheeks, ears, elbows, neck, hands, etc.* Also substitute other action words—*scrub, rub, dry,* and so forth. Explain the meaning of *squeaky clean.*

This Little Piggy

This little piggy went to market,

This little piggy stayed home,

This little piggy had roast beef,

This little piggy had none.

This little piggy went . . .

Wee, wee, wee,

All the way home!

SUGGESTION: Children probably remember this rhyme from early babyhood, when their parents grabbed each of their toes in succession as they said the lines of the poem. Now ask them to use finger movements—starting with the little finger, wiggle each one in succession and then wave the thumb while saying the last three lines. Let children replace *roast beef* with a favorite food of their own: *tacos, pizza, peanut butter*, etc. Or have them substitute other animals and change the sound made at the end accordingly.

This Old Man

This old man, he played one

He played knick-knack on his thumb

With a knick-knack paddywhack, give your dog a bone

This old man came rolling home

ADDITIONAL VERSES:

two—shoe	six—sticks
three—knee	seven—pen
four—door	eight—gate
five—hive	nine—spine
	ten—once again

SUGGESTION: This oral-language counting song will help children think about number words and words that rhyme with them. You may want to have children hold up a large numeral and/or word card at the appropriate verse.

Three Blind Mice

Three blind mice,

See how they run!

See how they run!

They all ran after the farmer's wife,

Who cut off their tails with a carving knife;

Did you ever see such a sight in your life

As three blind mice?

SUGGESTION: Children enjoy singing and talking about this song. A picture book by Janet Stevens, *Three Blind Mice*, reinforces the images.

Three Little Kittens

Three little kittens lost their mittens,
And they began to cry:
"Oh, Mother dear, we very much fear
Our mittens we have lost!"

"What, lost your mittens, you naughty kittens!
Then you shall have no pie."
"Meow, meow, meow, meow."
"No, you have shall have no pie."

The three little kittens found their mittens,
And they began to cry:
"Oh, Mother dear, see here, see here,
Our mittens we have found."

"What! Found your mittens? You good little kittens,
Now you shall have some pie."
"Purr, purr, purr, purr,
Purr, purr, purr."

SUGGESTION: Have children, individually or in small groups, say the dialogue of the mother and the kittens while everyone else says the rest. This poem lends itself to making a story map with pictures, one for each verse.

Three Men in a Tub

Rub-a-dub-dub,

Three men in a tub,

And who do you think were there?

The butcher, the baker,

The candlestick maker,

And all had come from the fair.

SUGGESTION: Have a small group of children say *rub-a-dub-dub* while the rest read the rhyme. You may need to discuss the meaning of *butcher, baker,* and *candlestick maker.*

fold
here

249

Time to Pick Up

Now it is time

To end our day.

Pick up our materials

And put them away.

SUGGESTION: Here is a rhyme to sing or say while cleaning the room. After learning this rhyme, invite children to say it with you as they clean up. Substitute more detailed words for *materials*: *blocks, puppets, crayons, papers.*

A Tisket, a Tasket

A tisket, a tasket,

A green and yellow basket.

I wrote a letter to my friend

And on my way I lost it.

I lost it, I lost it,

And on the way I lost it.

A little child picked it up,

And put it in her pocket.

Her pocket, her pocket,

She put it in her pocket.

A little child picked it up,

And put it in her pocket.

SUGGESTION: Have children play a game while reciting this rhyme. The child who is "it" skips around the outside of a circle of seated classmates carrying a basketful of "letters" (an easy word, a letter of the alphabet, someone's name), dropping one behind another child. This child jumps up, picks up the "letter," runs after the basket carrier, and tries to tag him or her. If the attempt is successful, the second child is "it" and gets the basket. Substitute children's names for *my friend* and *a little child*.

To Market, to Market

To market, to market,

To buy a fat pig.

Home again, home again,

Jiggety jig.

ADDITIONAL VERSES:
To market, to market,
To buy a fat hog.
Home again, home again,
Jiggety jog.

SUGGESTION: Have children draw and dictate or write how they might go to market and what they might buy. Have children recite the verse in various configurations, jumping up when they say the words *jiggety jig*.

Today

Today is Monday, today is Monday,

How are you, how are you?

Very well, I thank you,

Very well, I thank you,

How about you? How about you?

SUGGESTION: Have the children sing this verse to the tune of "Are You Sleeping?" Assign some to read the first two lines and others the response. Substitute the other days of the week to create another six verses.

Tommy Snooks

As Tommy Snooks and Bessy Brooks

Were walking out one Sunday,

Said Tommy Snooks to Bessy Brooks,

"Tomorrow will be Monday."

SUGGESTION: You can substitute children's names for *Tommy Snooks* and *Bessy Brooks*. This simple rhyme will help children remember the sequence of days in the week. Looking at the calendar, start on any day and have children figure out what *tomorrow* would be.

Tommy Thumbs

Tommy Thumbs up and

Tommy Thumbs down.

Tommy Thumbs dancing

All around the town.

Dancing on my shoulders.

Dancing on my head.

Dancing on my knees.

Now, tuck them into bed.

ACTIONS:
Tommy Thumbs up and [*thumbs-up sign*]
Tommy Thumbs down. [*both thumbs down*]
Tommy Thumbs dancing
All around the town. [*make thumbs dance*]
Dancing on my shoulders. [*dance thumbs on shoulders*]
Dancing on my head. [*dance thumbs on head*]
Dancing on my knees. [*dance thumbs on knees*]
Now, tuck them into bed. [*fold arms, hiding hands*]

SUGGESTION: Teach children to perform the accompanying actions. Repeat with the rest of the digits individually—*Peter Pointers, Toby Talls, Ringmen, Baby Fingers*—and then with all of them at once—*Finger Family.*

Toys Away

Toys away,

Toys away,

Time to put our

Toys away.

SUGGESTION: Have children chant this while they are putting things away. Substitute other words for *toys*, as appropriate: *blocks, books, coats,* etc.

Twinkle, Twinkle, Little Star

Twinkle, twinkle, little star,

How I wonder what you are!

Up above the world so high,

Like a diamond in the sky.

Twinkle, twinkle, little star,

How I wonder what you are!

SUGGESTION: Have the children sing the song. Substitute other words for *diamond* and illustrate the resulting poems with crayons. Create a new version of the poem together incorporating comical words and images, like this one by Lewis Carroll: *Twinkle, twinkle, little bat! | How I wonder what you're at! | Up above the world you fly, | Like a tea-tray in the sky. | Twinkle, twinkle, little bat! | How I wonder what you're at!*

Two, Four, Six, Eight

Two, four, six, eight,

Meet me at the garden gate.

If I'm late, do not wait,

Two, four, six, eight.

SUGGESTION: This rhyme has a strong beat. Have children use rhythm sticks or handclaps to mark each number word. After children have learned the rhyme, you may want to use a number line to show that they are skipping every other number. Another way to show the concept is to slow down and show the appropriate number of blocks.

Two Little Blackbirds

Two little blackbirds

Sitting on a hill,

One named Jack,

One named Jill.

Fly away, Jack,

Fly away, Jill.

Come back, Jack,

Come back, Jill.

ACTIONS:
Two little blackbirds [*both hands on shoulders*]
Sitting on a hill,
One named Jack, [*lift right hand above shoulder and put back down*]
One named Jill. [*lift left hand*]
Fly away, Jack, [*flutter right hand to reach up high*]
Fly away, Jill. [*flutter left hand to reach up high*]
Come back, Jack, [*bring right hand back to shoulder*]
Come back, Jill. [*bring left hand back to shoulder*]

SUGGESTION: Perform this poem as a finger play or puppet show. To make little puppets, attach cutout construction paper blackbirds to kraft sticks.

fold here

Two Little Houses

Two little houses,

Closed up tight.

Let's open the windows,

And let in some light.

ACTIONS:
Two little houses, [*make two fists*]
Closed up tight.
Let's open the windows, [*stick thumbs out*]
And let in some light. [*open hands*]

SUGGESTION: This simple finger play will be easy for children to learn. You can create a printed version with two houses that have windows that open. This is a good poem for shared reading.

Up in the North

Up in the North, a long way off,

A donkey got the whooping cough;

He whooped so hard with the whooping cough,

He whooped his head and tail right off.

SUGGESTION: Children will find this poem funny. They can say it several times, substituting the names of different animals.

fold
here

261

Up to the Ceiling

Up to the ceiling,

Down to the floor,

Left to the window,

Right to the door.

This is my right hand—

Raise it up high.

This is my left hand—

Reach for the sky.

Right hand, left hand,

Twirl them around.

Left hand, right hand,

Pound, pound, pound.

SUGGESTION: This rhyme gives children a good stretch break between activities and lets them practice distinguishing the left and right hands. The hand actions, in order, are: raise hands up, put hands down, point left with the left hand, point right with the right hand, raise right hand, raise left hand while keeping right hand up, twirl hands one around the other, and hit fists together three times.

Wash Hands, Wash

Wash hands, wash,

Daddy's gone to plow.

If you want your hands washed,

Wash them now.

VARIATION:
Warm hands, warm,
The men are gone to plow.
If you want to warm your hands,
Warm them now.

SUGGESTION: Assign half the children to read the first two lines and the other half to read the last two lines. You may need to discuss the meaning of *plow*.

We Can

We can jump, jump, jump,

We can hop, hop, hop,

We can clap, clap, clap,

We can stop, stop, stop.

We can nod our heads for yes,

We can shake our heads for no,

We can bend our knees a tiny bit,

And sit down very slow.

SUGGESTION: This is a good poem to use to help children move from one activity to another. Have them complete the actions as they say the words. Ask children to say the four words that end the lines in verse one. If they say them slowly, they can hear the /p/ at the end of each word. Create a print version of verse one and have children locate words that end in *p*.

Wee Willie Winkie

Wee Willie Winkie runs through the town,

Upstairs, downstairs, in his nightgown;

Rapping at the window,

Crying at the lock,

"Are the children all in bed?

For now it's eight o'clock!"

SUGGESTION: Children are fascinated by the image of Wee Willie Winkie running through the streets to check that all children are in bed. Tell them about the days when lamplighters lit the streetlights at night. Substitute other times for *eight o'clock* and other names for *Willie Winkie*. Children can say *Wee Willie Winkie* and notice that the words sound the same at the beginning.

fold
here

265

What Animals Say

Little pup, little pup,

What do you say?

"Woof, woof, woof!

Let's go and play."

ADDITIONAL VERSES:

Kittycat, kittycat,
How about you?
"Meow, meow, meow!
And I purr, too."

Pretty bird, pretty bird,
Have you a song?
"Tweet, tweet, tweet!
The whole day long."

Jersey cow, jersey cow,
What do you do?
"Moo, moo, moo!
And give milk, too."

Little lamb, little lamb,
What do you say?
"Baa, baa, baa!
Can Mary play?"

SUGGESTION: Recite this poem as a game. Have one child recite the first rhymed question and choose a classmate to answer it. This child then chooses someone to ask the next question. Begin with one or two animals used over and over, but expand as children learn more verses. Children who are chosen have to pick up the cue from the first two lines and respond as the appropriate animal.

What's the Weather?

What's the weather?

What's the weather?

What's the weather like today?

Is it rainy?

Is it windy?

Are there clouds or is there sun?

ADDITIONAL VERSES:
It is _____.
It is _____.
That's the weather today.
Today, it is _____.
It is _____ today.

SUGGESTION: Sing this to the tune of "Clementine." You might want to sing this in the morning as children are arriving as a weather check. Half the group can sing the question (which remains the same) while the other half sings the response (which changes with the weather).

Wheels on the Bus

The wheels on the bus

Go 'round and 'round,

'Round and 'round,

'Round and 'round,

The wheels on the bus

Go 'round and 'round

All around the town.

ADDITIONAL VERSES:

The wipers on the bus
Go swish, swish, swish,
Swish, swish, swish,
Swish, swish, swish,
The wipers on the bus
Go swish, swish, swish
All around the town.

The driver on the bus
Calls, "Move on back!"
"Move on back!"
"Move on back!"
The driver on the bus
Calls, "Move on back!"
All around the town.

The people on the bus
Get up and down,
Up and down,
Up and down,
The people on the bus
Get up and down
All around the town.

The horn on the bus
Goes beep, beep, beep,
Beep, beep, beep,
Beep, beep, beep,
The horn on the bus
Goes beep, beep, beep
All around the town.

The baby on the bus
Cries, "Wah, wah, wah"
"Wah, wah, wah."
"Wah, wah, wah."
The baby on the bus
Cries, "Wah, wah, wah"
All around the town.

The parents on the bus
Go, "Shh, shh, shh,"
"Shh, shh, shh,"
"Shh, shh, shh,"
The parents on the bus
Go, "Shh, shh, shh"
All around the town.

SUGGESTION: Children love pantomiming the motions and making representative onomatopoeic sounds as they sing or recite each verse. They can put chairs in a "bus" pattern with one child using an imaginary wheel to "drive" the bus. Help them create some new verses: *the lights go blink, blink, blink; the door goes open/shut; the dogs on the bus go bark, bark, bark.* Several picture books are based on this song, *The Wheels on the Bus: Traditional Song,* by Paul O. Zelinsky. Mary Kovalski's *The Wheels on the Bus* extends the ideas of the song and tells a different story. Lenny Hort's book *The Seals on the Bus* is a humorous adaptation.

When Ducks Get Up in the Morning

When ducks get up in the morning,

They always say, "Quack, Quack."

When ducks get up in the morning,

They always say, "Quack, quack.

Quack, quack, quack, quack, quack, quack."

They always say, "Quack, quack."

SUGGESTION: Substitute other animals and sounds to create more verses: *birds—tweet, tweet; cows—moo, moo; cats—meow, meow; dogs—bow-wow; sheep—baa, baa; pigs—oink, oink.*

fold
here

269

Where Is Thumbkin?

Where is thumbkin?

Where is thumbkin?

Here I am.

Here I am.

How are you today, sir?

Very well, I thank you.

Run away.

Run away.

ACTIONS:

Where is thumbkin? [*hands behind back*]

Where is thumbkin?

Here I am. [*show one thumb*]

Here I am. [*show other thumb*]

How are you today, sir? [*bend one thumb toward the other*]

Very well, I thank you. [*bend opposite thumb in response, as if talking*]

Run away. [*return one thumb and hand behind back*]

Run away. [*return other thumb and hand behind back*]

SUGGESTION: Sing this song to the tune of "Are You Sleeping?" Have children act out the whole story. Extend the rhyme by substituting all the other digits, one at a time: *Where is pointer? Tall one? Ring finger? Pinkie?* As a variation, have children sit in a circle. Substitute a child's name for *thumbkin* as you sing the first two lines. The named child sings lines 3 and 4; you sing line 5; child sings lines 6, 7, and 8 and begins verse again using another child's name.

Who Is Wearing Red?

Oh, who is wearing red?

Oh, who is wearing red?

Please tell me if you can,

Oh, who is wearing red?

Oh, _____ is wearing red

Oh, _____ is wearing red

That's the color of her _____.

Oh, _____ is wearing red

SUGGESTION: Sung to the tune of "The Farmer in the Dell," insert children's name in the blank spaces after *Oh*, and the name of the article of clothing in the third line of the response. Using this song in a pocket chart allows you to insert name cards and color words.

fold here

271

Who Stole the Cookies?

Who stole the cookies

from the cookie jar?

_____ stole the cookies

from the cookie jar.

Who, me?

Yes, you.

Couldn't be.

Then, who?

SUGGESTION: Use this rhyme to play a circle game, substituting different children's names each time. The child whose name is used reads *Who me?* and *Couldn't be* and then starts the rhyme again, inserting another child's name. A variation is to hold up a name card instead of saying the name orally. Pair this poem with the picture book *Who Took the Cookies from the Cookie Jar?* by Bonnie Lass, illustrated by Ashley Wolff.

The Whole Duty of Children

by Robert Louis Stevenson

A child should always say what's true,

And speak when he is spoken to,

And behave mannerly at table:

At least as far as he is able.

SUGGESTION: Invite the children to discuss what good manners are in your classroom. Turn the poem into a list through interactive writing *(tell the truth, listen and answer, clean up your materials)*.

fold
here

273

Whoops, Johnny

Johnny, Johnny, Johnny, Johnny,

Whoops, Johnny,

Whoops, Johnny,

Johnny, Johnny, Johnny, Johnny.

SUGGESTION: Make a game out of this poem: using the index finger of the right hand, say *Johnny* while tapping the top of each finger of the opposite hand, beginning with the pinky. Then slide the right index finger from the top of the left index finger down along the curve to the top of the thumb. Repeat the action in reverse for the last two lines. You can also substitute other children's names.

Why Rabbits Jump

"Why are you rabbits jumping so?

Now please tell why, tell why."

"We jump to see the big round moon

Up in the sky, the sky."

SUGGESTION: Divide the group into two and have half of the children read the first two lines and the others read the final two lines. Let some children be rabbits and jump every time they hear the word *jump*. Take turns.

Willaby, Wallaby, Woo

Willaby, wallaby, woo,

An elephant stepped on you.

Willaby, wallaby, wee,

An elephant stepped on me.

SUGGESTION: Children love to act out this rhyme. Change *woo* to words that rhyme with children's names: *Willaby, wallaby, wason, / An elephant stepped on Jason; Willaby, wallaby, wackie, / An elephant stepped on Jackie;* and so forth. The sillier the rhymes, the more intriguing the verse.

The Wind

I can blow like the wind.

I can bring the rain.

When I blow very softly,

I can whisper my name.

SUGGESTION: Children can create the sounds of wind and rain and then whisper their own names.

Wind the Bobbin

Wind, wind, wind the bobbin,

Wind, wind, wind, the bobbin,

Pull, pull, clap! clap! clap!

ACTIONS:
Wind, wind, wind the bobbin, [*turn hands around*]
Wind, wind, wind, the bobbin, [*turn hands around*]
Pull, pull, [*pull hands from center out*]
clap! clap! clap! [*clap three times*]

SUGGESTION: Discuss what a bobbin is and how it is used, and bring in a sewing machine bobbin for the children to look at. Have children make winding hand motions as they say the poem.

Window Watching

See the window I have here,

So big and wide and square.

I can stand in front of it,

And see the things out there.

SUGGESTION: Add hand movements—drawing a square in the air for lines 1 and 2 and shading the eyes as if looking in the distance for lines 3 and 4. Ask children to draw large windows with themselves inside, looking out at whatever their imagination comes up with. They can label what they see. You might also post a copy of the poem next to a window in your classroom.

fold
here

Windshield Wiper

I'm a windshield wiper.

This is how I go:

Back and forth, back and forth,

In the rain and snow.

SUGGESTION: Have children enact this poem by moving one or both arms as they chant. (Bend arm at elbow, fingers pointing up; move arm left and right, pivoting at the elbow.) They can vary the tempo to indicate different kinds of weather. Feature the poem with a picture of windshield wipers on a poetry chart.

Yankee Doodle

Yankee Doodle came to town,

Riding on a pony;

He stuck a feather in his cap

And called it macaroni.

SUGGESTION: Children may find it interesting that *macaroni* used to mean fashionable, stylish, or pretty rather than the macaroni you eat.

fold
here

281

Zoom, Zoom, Zoom

Zoom, zoom, zoom,

I'm going to the moon.

If you want to take a trip,

Climb aboard my rocket ship.

Zoom, zoom, zoom,

I'm going to the moon.

ACTIONS:

Zoom, zoom, zoom, [*brush hands together in an upward motion*]
I'm going to the moon. [*brush hands together again, sending the top hand very high*]
If you want to take a trip,
Climb aboard my rocket ship. [*pantomime climbing a ladder*]
Zoom, zoom, zoom, [*brush hands together in an upward motion*]
I'm going to the moon. [*brush hands together again, sending the top hand very high*]

SUGGESTION: Have children make the hand movements as they recite the poem. As an alternative, have one child sit in a row of chairs as you say the poem. At the end he chooses another child to join him and the poem begins again, adding up to four or five children.